To the memory of
Michael Griffiths and Terry Jackson

Language Teaching:
A Scheme for Teacher Education

Editors: C N Candlin and H G Widdowson

Vocabulary

Michael McCarthy

Oxford University Press
1990

Oxford University Press
Walton Street, Oxford OX2 6DP

Oxford New York Toronto
Delhi Bombay Calcutta Madras Karachi
Petaling Jaya Singapore Hong Kong Tokyo
Nairobi Dar es Salaam Cape Town
Melbourne Auckland

and associated companies in
Berlin Ibadan

OXFORD and OXFORD ENGLISH
are trade marks of Oxford University Press

ISBN 0 19 437136 0

Typeset by Wyvern Typesetting Ltd, Bristol

Printed in Great Britain by Thomson Litho Ltd, East Kilbride, Scotland

Contents

The author and series editors

Michael McCarthy is a lecturer in Modern English Language in the Department of English Studies at the University of Nottingham, having previously been a lecturer in Applied English Linguistics in the School of English at the University of Birmingham. He has also taught English in several countries and travels extensively, lecturing on vocabulary and discourse analysis.

Christopher N. Candlin is Professor of Linguistics in the School of English and Linguistics at Macquarie University, Sydney, and Director of the National Centre for English Language Teaching and Research, having previously been Professor of Applied Linguistics and Director of the Centre for Language in Social Life at the University of Lancaster. He also co-founded and directed the Institute for English Language Education at Lancaster, where he worked on issues in in-service education for teachers.

Henry Widdowson is Professor of English for Speakers of Other Languages at the University of London Institute of Education, having previously been Lecturer in Applied Linguistics at the University of Edinburgh. Before that, he worked on materials development and teacher education as a British Council English Language Officer in Sri Lanka and Bangladesh.

Through work with The British Council, The Council of Europe, and other agencies, both Editors have had extensive and varied experience of language teaching, teacher education, and curriculum development overseas, and both contribute to seminars, conferences, and professional journals.

Introduction

Vocabulary

It is the experience of most language teachers that the single, biggest component of any language course is vocabulary. No matter how well the student learns grammar, no matter how successfully the sounds of L2 are mastered, without words to express a wide range of meanings, communication in an L2 just cannot happen in any meaningful way. And yet vocabulary often seems to be the least systematized and the least well catered for of all the aspects of learning a foreign language. The purpose of this book is to look at what we do know about the vocabulary of a language like English and to reflect on how this has been applied in language teaching.

In Section One we look at theoretical, descriptive, and psycholinguistic models of the vocabulary of English. We consider to what extent the vast word-store of English can be said to be organized, whether in terms of the systematic semantic relations among words, or how words are organized in the mind, or how words are patterned in their actual use by speakers and writers of the language.

Section Two considers how the insights of Section One have been translated into vocabulary teaching materials and lexical reference works. It attempts to get below the surface of published materials to trace the links between them and the theoretical and descriptive models that have informed them (whether consciously or only subconsciously as general trends in language teaching have changed) from an emphasis on simply teaching facts about language systems to language as communication, to language learning as an interactive process, and towards individualization.

Section Three consists entirely of tasks designed to take the insights of Sections One and Two into the classroom, where teachers can explore for themselves the relevance of theory and description. The emphasis is on involving the learner in such explorations, and on evaluating the activities in one's own teaching situation.

During the preparation of this book I was greatly inspired by the careful editorship of the series editors. In particular, Professor Henry Widdowson gave a lot of his time without complaint to clearing the fog that inevitably descends over the author's mind from time to time, and which seeps into the manuscript here and there. Any fog that remains, and any other shortcomings, are entirely my responsibility. Stuart Redman has also been most helpful, contributing ideas in discussion and sharpening my own, as have colleagues in the English Departments of Birmingham and Nottingham Universities. Seven years of MA students at Birmingham also have their part in this book; at some time or other, most of it has been tried on them and invaluable feedback received. Above all, two longstanding mentors of mine on lexis, John Sinclair of Birmingham and Tony Cowie of Leeds, have continued to inspire me and make me think it was all worthwhile. Jeanne McCarten has never complained of the hours the book has taken me away from our domestic life and has also contributed a number of invaluable ideas. To all these people and many more go all my thanks.

Michael McCarthy

Language Teaching:
A Scheme for Teacher Education

The purpose of this scheme of books is to engage language teachers in a process of continual professional development. We have designed it so as to guide teachers towards the critical appraisal of ideas and the informed application of these ideas in their own classrooms. The scheme provides the means for teachers to take the initiative themselves in pedagogic planning. The emphasis is on critical enquiry as a basis for effective action.

We believe that advances in language teaching stem from the independent efforts of teachers in their own classrooms. This independence is not brought about by imposing fixed ideas and promoting fashionable formulas. It can only occur where teachers, individually or collectively, explore principles and experiment with techniques. Our purpose is to offer guidance on how this might be achieved.

The scheme consists of three sub-series of books covering areas of enquiry and practice of immediate relevance to language teaching and learning. Sub-series 1 (of which this present volume forms a part) focuses on areas of *language knowledge*, with books linked to the conventional levels of linguistic description: pronunciation, vocabulary, grammar, and discourse. Sub-series 2 focuses on different *modes of behaviour* which realize this knowledge. It is concerned with the pedagogic skills of speaking, listening, reading, and writing. Sub-series 3 focuses on a variety of *modes of action* which are needed if this knowledge and behaviour is to be acquired in the operation of language teaching. The books in this sub-series have to do with such topics as syllabus design, the content of language course, and aspects of methodology and evaluation.

This sub-division of the field is not meant to suggest that different topics can be dealt with in isolation. On the contrary, the concept of a scheme implies making coherent links between all these different areas of enquiry and activity. We wish to emphasize how their integration formalizes the complex factors present in any teaching process. Each book, then, highlights a particular topic, but also deals contingently with other issues, themselves treated as focal in other books in the series. Clearly, an enquiry into a mode of behaviour like speaking, for example, must also refer to aspects of language knowledge which it realizes. It must also connect to modes of action which can be directed at developing this behaviour in learners. As elements of the whole scheme, therefore, books cross-refer both within and across the different sub-series.

This principle of cross-reference which links the elements of the scheme is also applied to the internal design of the different inter-related books within it. Thus, each book contains three sections, which, by a combination of text and task, engage the reader in a principled enquiry into ideas and practices. The first section of each book makes explicit those theoretical ideas which bear on the topic in question. It provides a conceptual framework for those sections which follow. Here the text has a mainly *explanatory* function, and the tasks serve to clarify and consolidate the points raised. The second section shifts the focus of attention to how the ideas from Section One relate to activities in the classroom. Here the text is concerned with *demonstration*, and the tasks are designed to get readers to evaluate suggestions for teaching in reference both to the ideas from Section One and also to their own teaching experience. In the third section this experience is projected into future work. Here the set of tasks, modelled on those in Section Two, are designed to be carried out by the reader as a combination of teaching techniques and action research in the actual classroom. It is this section that renews the reader's contact with reality: the ideas expounded in Section One and linked to pedagogic practice in Section Two are now to be systematically *tested out* in the process of classroom teaching.

If language teaching is to be a genuinely professional enterprise, it requires continual experimentation and evaluation on the part of practitioners whereby in seeking to be more effective in their pedagogy they provide at the same time—and as a corollary—for their own continuing education. It is our aim in this scheme to promote this dual purpose.

Christopher N. Candlin
Henry Widdowson

Explaining vocabulary

1 Words

1.1 Introduction

It is very daunting to be reminded that the vocabulary of a language like English consists of several hundred thousand words. How can language teachers and learners approach this vast, seemingly endless store of language and make sense of it? To even attempt to do so, we need satisfying answers to the following questions:

1 How is the vocabulary composed? What sorts of elements does it contain?

2 Is the vocabulary of a language organized or is it just a gigantic list of items, every one unique?

3 If it is organized, can we use its structuring principles in language teaching in a way similar to the way we utilize the regularity and organization of grammatical structure?

4 How can anything so vast as the vocabulary of a language, particularly a second language, or even a relatively small part of it, be acquired by the human mind, stored, and made retrievable when required?

Our answers to these questions may not be definitive or complete, but even if we can only partially answer them, the answers may offer the prospect of a more rigorous approach to vocabulary teaching.

1.2 Word-formation

When we speak of the vocabulary of a language we are speaking primarily, but not exclusively, of the *words* of that language. For our purposes here, it is most convenient to think of words as freestanding items of language that have meaning. If we take the English word 'eating', we can see that it is freestanding in itself, and that within it it has another potentially freestanding element 'eat', independently meaningful from the second element '-ing', which is meaningful but *bound*, that is, not freestanding. There is an English word 'eat', but there is no English word '-ing'. The two meaningful parts of 'eating' are called *morphemes*; therefore we can say that a word must consist of at least one potentially freestanding morpheme. Some words may consist of several morphemes: 'deformed' consists of three—'de-form-ed'—only 'form' is a word in its own right. However, 'wastepaper-basket' consists of three morphemes which at the same time are capable of being three freestanding words in other contexts. From this it is clear that when we talk of learning *words* in a language sometimes we mean either single morphemes or *roots*, such as 'laugh', 'make', 'box', and 'window' which cannot be further subdivided, or roots with bound morphemes attached either at the beginning as *prefixes* or at the end as *suffixes*, such as 're-make' and 'laughter' (*derived words*), and sometimes we mean items that consist of more than one root but which have a single identity in that they name a single thing or concept, such as 'make-believe', 'window-dressing', and 'jack-in-the-box' (*compound words*). For the fullest account of English word-formation processes, see Bauer (1983). Recognizing the composition of words is important; the learner can go a long way towards deciphering new words if he or she can see familiar morphemes within them.

▶ TASK 1

How many morphemes are there in each of these words? Are the words roots, derived words, or compounds?

hundred	*singer*	*finger*	*workforce*
freeze-dry	*mismatch*	*complexity*	*bin*
troublemaker	*irregularity*	*feature*	*pathfinder*
imposing	*impossible*		

Sometimes, recognizing morphemes is not so easy. When morphemes combine to form words, sound changes and/or spelling changes can disguise them, making their presence less obvious to the untrained ear or eye. 'Reduce' changes its vowel sound to 'reduction' when it becomes a noun; 'dry' and 'dried' have the same vowel sound but the spelling changes. Irregular verb-forms are another example of this: 'sang' must be related to 'sing' and 'sung', while 'went' seems quite unconnected with 'go' or 'gone'. 'Beauty' changes its spelling in 'beautiful'. Sometimes such changes are recurrent: the /k/ sound in 'electric' becomes /s/ in 'electricity'; the same pattern holds good for 'authentic' → 'authenticity'; 'domestic' → 'domesticity', and 'public' → 'publicity'. The stress change from the adjective 'pérfect' to the verb 'perféct' is typical of a whole group of stress-changing words (e.g. 'an óbject' → 'to objéct'; 'a décrease' → 'to decréase'). Where regularities of this kind can be observed, they can be capitalized upon by teachers and learners tackling the problems of word-recognition in written and spoken contexts.

▶ TASK 2

Separate the words below into the morphemes that compose them and consider what problems of analysis, or recognition, or of relating them to other forms of the same word a learner might have with them. For example:

word: *redemption*
morphemes: *redeem* + noun suffix *-tion*
problem(s): recognizing that *redem(p)* is a variant of *redeem*

plentiful   dismayed   disappoint   include   ridden   strode

Studying how words are formed offers one way of classifying vocabulary for teaching and learning purposes, for example, presenting together words that are alike in *structure*, though not necessarily in meaning, such as derived adjectives ending in '-al' (e.g. 'brutal', 'frontal', and 'horizontal'). This is not, of course, the only way of organizing vocabulary for teaching but it is undoubtedly useful as an aid to memorizing words in some cases, especially where small, manageable sets of words with morphemic similarities can be isolated. Most teachers already do this with irregular verbs that follow a set pattern, for example, those that have /ɪ/, /æ/, /ʌ/ in their three main parts (e.g. 'drink', 'drank', 'drunk'; 'ring', 'rang', 'rung'; 'sink', 'sank', 'sunk') but the same could be done, for example, with those adjectives occurring with the relatively infrequent prefix 'a-', meaning 'an absence of . . .', as in 'asocial', 'apolitical', 'asexual', 'amoral', and the element of shared meaning involved in these words, or any other recurring pattern.

The principles of word-formation can be looked at in two different ways. One is simply to consider them as part of the rule-systems of the language, and to describe them for learners in the way that we describe and explain grammatical rules or pronunciation rules. But we can also look at word-formation as a resource in the language, something the learner should be allowed to experiment with and use strategically. We might consider, for example, isolating a small group of highly productive prefixes or suffixes and encouraging learners to create 'new' words. Some of their creations will probably be words that already exist in the language, and some will be non-established words. This latter group need not be jettisoned, but can be explored for literary value, humorous potential, or simply for filling 'gaps' in the language (see **2.3**). English, for example, is only just beginning to use a compound equivalent to the well-established Swedish compound adjective '*miljövänlig*' ('*miljö-vänlig*'), literally 'environment-friendly', for products and processes that do not damage the environment, up till recently a concept only expressible as a clause in English. Creative word-formation can also be seen as a communicative strategy, for supplying formations when the right word cannot be found. Possible ways of exploiting word-formation will be examined and evaluated in Section Two of this book.

▶ TASK 3

What do the words in each group have in common in terms of changes in spelling, stress, or pronunciation when they change from one word-class to another?

Group 1: change these nouns to adjectives
   malice   finance   office   space

Group 2: change these verbs to nouns
   record   contest   protest   increase

Group 3: change these verbs to a noun expressing 'doer' or agent
   create   invigilate   donate   liberate

1.3 Multi-word units

So far we have talked of only three types of unit in the vocabulary of a language like English: basic roots (e.g. 'plate'), derived words (e.g. 'defrost'), and compounds (e.g. 'lampshade'), but when we look at written and spoken texts in English, we see a large number of recurring fixed forms which consist of more than one word yet which are not syntactically the same as compounds. One familiar type of fixed form is the *idiom*. Let us take the idiom 'to bite the dust' meaning 'to die'. It is fixed, like a fossilized chunk of language, insomuch as what the speaker can do with it is limited. We can say 'he bit the dust', but not (without producing a highly marked utterance) 'I think he deserves a dust-biting': we cannot say 'he chewed the dust' or 'he bit some dust' without radically changing the meaning of the idiom. Its 'idiomaticity' is partly identified by its fixedness; there is no sensible way in which this fossilized block can be carved up into smaller pieces for language teaching; it should clearly be treated just like basic roots, derived words, and compounds, that is to say, as a single *lexical item* even though, in its internal structure, it is a clause, with a verb and an object. All languages are rich in idioms and specialized idiom dictionaries are available (e.g. for English, Cowie and Mackin 1975; Cowie, Mackin, and McCaig 1983; Longman 1979). Idioms can often be grouped together according to form (Cowie and Mackin 1975, brings together verbs and particles). In English, one recurring type is the *verb + the + object* idiom, as in:

to bite the dust
to kick the bucket
to pass the buck

Certain verbs seem to be 'idiom-prone' and regularly partake in the formation of idioms, for example, as with 'go' and 'make':

to go mad	to make the best of
to go west	to make money
to go off	to make something of
to go wild	to make off with
to go easy	to make something up

▶ TASK 4

1 Can you add more idioms to lists A and B that are similar in form to the examples given?

A *verb + the + object*
  to bite the dust
  to take the mickey
  to hit the sack

B *to be + prepositional phrase*
  to be out on a limb
  to be in the know
  to be on the ball

2 Can you complete the idioms in this list?

  to be + as + adjective + as + noun
  to be as daft as a brush
  to be as dead as . . .
  to be as clear as . . .
  to be as clean as . . .
  to be as bold as . . .
  to be as flat as . . .
  to be as keen as . . .

If you have difficulty, consult the *Oxford Dictionary of Current Idiomatic English*, *Volume 2* (Cowie, Mackin, and McCaig 1983).

Grouping on formal lines may have mnemonic value (i.e. it may facilitate memorization) but it does not solve the problem that the meaning of an idiom, if not already known, is only retrievable from context, since analysis of the elements of an idiom may be at best only partially helpful and at worst utterly misleading. But, as with single words, grouping together items of similar structure should not be dismissed out of hand; good learners use all devices at their disposal to absorb vocabulary. Linguistic descriptions of different kinds can help by offering various organizing principles for what otherwise might seem a depressingly endless task.

Idioms vary from being opaque in their meaning (e.g. 'to kick the bucket' contains no clues as to its idiomatic meaning of 'to die'), to being semiopaque ('to pass the buck' can be paraphrased as 'to pass the responsibility'), to being relatively transparent ('to see the light' meaning 'to understand' is a phrase most learners of English do not find too bewildering). But 'to see the light' would still qualify as a frozen chunk of language, just as 'to bite the dust' does. (*'Suddenly I saw the lamp' and *'we need more light-seeing here' are not permissible forms. I have used the convention, here and elsewhere in this book, of marking such forms with an asterisk.) Idioms can sometimes seem less problematic because they share features that occur widely in other languages; for example, using an animal as an object of comparison in an idiomatic phrase is very common among the languages of the world (Makkai 1978). German, for instance, seems to have almost as many (but often not overlapping) idioms involving 'cat' and 'dog' as English does, but there might still be difficulties caused by different associative meanings for particular animals in different cultures (Arabic perceptions of cats and dogs are different from British perceptions, for example).

Idioms are only one type of *multi-word unit* found in the vocabularies of languages. *Binomials* (and occasionally *trinomials*) are another. These are pairs and trios of words which display fixed membership and sequence and which, like idioms, should be treated as single vocabulary items. English has the following:

binomials	*trinomials*
back to front	cool, calm, and collected
wine and dine	ready, willing, and able
to and fro	morning, noon, and night
fish and chips	hook, line, and sinker
ladies and gentlemen	lock, stock, and barrel
in and out	
back and forth	
clean and tidy	
sick and tired	

Many of these exist in other languages, but sometimes with a reversal of order (e.g. '*tuan-tuan dan puan-puan*' = 'gentlemen and ladies' in Malay, rather than 'ladies and gentlemen' as in English; see Carter and McCarthy 1988:25).

▶ TASK 5

Translate the following English phrases into another language known to you, or, alternatively, use a dictionary or a native-speaker informant to get a translation. Does the foreign language translation match the English word for word, or are there differences in word-order, or in the words used, or in how they are joined?

back and forth	We searched high and low.
ladies and gentlemen	I go there now and then.
black-and-white film	We talked about this and that.
from head to foot	

It will be clear by now that we are proposing quite a broad view of vocabulary. If the vocabulary is to include compounds, idioms, and binomials as well as single words, then there are many other phenomena which may be included too. We noted earlier that some idioms were more opaque than others; if we look further at the relationship between opacity of meaning and fixedness of form, we find that even quite transparent phrases are often fixed in their syntax.

Consider these phrases with 'talk':

to talk turkey	*opaque*
to talk shop	↑
to talk business	↓
to talk politics	*transparent*

There seems to be a scale of opacity: 'to talk politics' is transparent but still syntactically fixed. We might not want to call it an 'idiom' at all, but we would probably still consider it as a useful chunk for the learner to learn. We then realize that hundreds of chunks operate in the same way: the phrase 'a thing of the past' is transparent but fixed. Sometimes, quite long clauses are fixed and come ready-made, for example, the catchphrase 'they don't make them like that any more'. This is a particularly good example of this widespread phenomenon: it has regular syntax and no odd vocabulary items within it, yet the morphemes that compose it are as fixed and untransposable as the morphemes of many compounds and single words. Alexander (1978) identifies a whole series of fixed items regularly used in conversation, including *gambits* ('first of all'; 'let's face it'), *links* ('that reminds me'; 'another thing'), *responders* ('I guessed as much'; 'you must be joking'), and *closers* ('nice talking to you'; 'I'd better go now'). These all display that same ready-made unity that idioms and other fixed phrases possess. The broad view of vocabulary will include them in its entries, and the entries will be not words, but lexical items, some of which will be single words and some of which will be multi-word units.

▶ **TASK 6**

Consider the following sentences from the point of view of opacity or transparency of the italicized phrases. Which would be more problematic for a learner of English? Rank them in order of difficulty and note what the difficulties might be for a learner.

1 He *drinks like a fish*.
2 It's time *to ring the changes* in this office.
3 Please don't *make a scene* about it.
4 Women have *made their voices heard* in recent years in more and more areas of life.
5 That examination was *kid's stuff*.
6 I've been playing football since I was *knee-high to a grasshopper*.
7 He thinks he's got the job, but *I know different*.
8 Hi! *Long time no see!* How are you?

Some idioms are more invariable than others. When someone 'passes the buck', we can indeed comment 'this is a case of buck-passing', but when someone has died we cannot say *'this is a case of bucket-kicking', even though such an expression is grammatically well-formed. What can or cannot be done to one fixed form, in terms of substituting items or transposing items, is not necessarily true for any other. This is naturally a great problem for anyone learning a foreign language, and knowing what the possibilities are is a skill that comes with observation and practice. At this stage of our enquiry, it is sufficient to note that multi-word units (or *lexical phrases*—see Nattinger 1988 and also Bygate: *Speaking*, in this Scheme) are extremely common in language and that the view that vocabulary study is only concerned with single words is inadequate. In Section Two we shall consider how these multi-word items are dealt with in teaching materials.

► TASK 7

Look at this piece of natural conversational data and identify common lexical phrases used by the speakers which you consider could be usefully treated as single items for vocabulary teaching/learning purposes:

A: I don't know whether you have talked with Hilary about the diary situation.
B: well, she has been explaining to me in rather more general terms what you are sort of doing and . . .
A: what it was all about, yes
B: I gather you've been at it for nine years
A: by golly that's true, yes, yes, it's not a long time of course in this . . . in this sort of work you know
B: well, but it's quite a long time by any standards
A: yes, suppose so
B: she told me what you did and we decided we were both a bit out of date compared with present-day students and . . .
A: well, I suppose that's true . . .
(Svartvik and Quirk 1980:408)

The presence of multi-word units in natural data is so common that it has led one linguist, Sinclair (1987), to suggest that what he calls 'the idiom principle', the use of ready-made chunks such as those we have been examining, may well be the basic organizing principle in language production. In turn, this suggests that the construction of free phrases 'from scratch' may form a less important part of oral production than we think (see also Bolinger 1976).

2 Lexical relations

2.1 Collocation

There is another binding force between the words of a language which is distinct from the fixed syntax of idioms and other phrases. In English we can say 'she has a beige car' but not *'she has beige hair'; I can say 'she has blond hair' but not *'she has a blond car'. 'Beige' and 'blond', although both describing colours, are restricted in respect of what words they may combine with. 'Beige' collocates with 'car' but not with 'hair'; 'blond' collocates with 'hair' but not with 'car'. The relationship of *collocation* is fundamental in the study of vocabulary; it is a marriage contract between words, and some words are more firmly married to each other than others. It is an important organizing principle in the vocabulary of any language. The relationship between 'blond' and 'hair' is extremely *strong* (given 'blond', I can hardly be talking of anything else but 'hair'); 'brown hair' is a different kind of relationship, one that is relatively *weak* ('brown' and 'hair' may both combine with a large number of other words). The word 'the' may collocate with virtually any noun and is therefore such a weak collocator that we can hardly make any useful collocational statement about it and we would thus want to leave it to the grammar book to describe its functions. However, the division between grammar and lexis is not so sharp as the last remark might suggest: any word in the language can be examined from the point of view of grammar, and, vice-versa, any word, even words like articles and prepositions, can be considered as vocabulary items.

Languages are full of strong collocational pairs and, therefore, collocation deserves to be a central aspect of vocabulary study. Let us consider some simple, everyday words denoting size, and see how they collocate with a random selection of single nouns:

	problem	amount	shame	man
large	?	√	×	√
great	√	√	√	√
big	√	√	×	√
major	√	?	×	×

√ = collocates   ? = questionable   × = does not collocate

Table 1

The table shows three things: that some collocations are perfectly normal, or *unmarked* (the ticks); that some would be felt to be unusual, or *marked* but still acceptable (the question marks), and that some would be considered very highly marked or *unacceptable* (the crosses). The table also shows a more complex feature of collocability: 'big shame' is a doubtful collocation in English, but 'great big shame' seems much more acceptable; collocation may often be more than just which *pairs* of words can occur together and may govern longer stretches of language.

► **TASK 8**

Fill in the matrix. Indicate normal collocations with a tick (√); doubtful or unusual ones with a question mark (?), and unacceptable ones with a cross (×).

	a laugh	*a smoke*	*an experience*	*a trip*
take				
make				
have				
do				

Knowledge of collocational appropriacy is part of the native speaker's competence, and can be problematic for learners in cases where collocability is language-specific and does not seem solely determined by universal semantic constraints (such that 'green blood' would be odd in any human culture). Even very advanced learners often make inappropriate or unacceptable collocations.

► **TASK 9**

Here are some examples of sentences written by learners of English. Identify any odd or unacceptable collocations and suggest alternatives:

1 His books commanded criticism from many people.
2 There was a high difference between the two teams.
3 I am doing this exam because I want to achieve a step in my career.
4 He had been found guilty of some slight crimes.
5 She won many competitions, forming fame in the process.
6 I was very grateful, because he had rescued my life.

Knowledge of collocation is knowledge of what words are most likely to occur together. It is therefore a question of typicality and statements about collocation can never be absolute (see Halliday 1966). The notion of typicality is important, for without it we could not recognize untypical collocations, which are part of the creativity and the imaginative dimension we find in literature. Modern poetry often relies on collocating the unusual, as this extract shows:

The puffins sit in a book: the muffins are molten:
The crass clock chimes,
Timely the hour and deserved.

(Lawrence Durrell: 'The Death of General Uncebunke')

Collocations such as 'muffins/molten', 'crass/clock', and 'deserved/hour' are extremely unusual, and their unusualness is part of the force of the poem. Similarly, advertising language and other sorts of persuasive language often use marked or unusual collocations such as slogans to catch the eye or ear: compare the typical collocation 'sky-blue' with the untypical 'galaxy-blue', the name of one of the shades of blue currently available for Ford cars. Recognizing untypical collocations is often a problem for the language learner, even though the phenomenon will occur in the learner's L1 too, and subtle layers of meaning in texts may be lost.

It will be noted that, in talking about collocations in the poetry extract, we were not necessarily dealing with adjacent words; the collocational relationship still applies, even though several words may separate the collocating items. In this sense, collocational pairs are different from compounds, where words are syntactically bound to one another too. The following extracts from a newspaper report concerning a planning application for a new shopping centre show collocation at work over clause-boundaries (strong collocations are in italics):

'The study of planning *appeals* for similar centres in the past, most of which were *rejected*, suggests that the future is more hopeful for developers . . . Now that the Secretary of State for the Environment has said that *applications* should be *approved* unless there are good reasons against them, many more should *succeed*.'
(*Independent*, 10 October 1986)

The collocational relationship between 'reject/appeal' and 'application/approve/succeed' is strong, despite the intervening words. The relationship could appear in a variety of syntactic realizations:

1 They rejected my appeal.
   The rejection of his appeal was a great shock.
2 My application succeeded.
   She made a successful application.
   Getting our application approved took ages.
   You have to submit your application for approval.

One text alone does not permit us to make a general statement about the collocation of 'application' with words like 'submit' and 'approve'; our knowledge that they do collocate is based on years of experience of masses of data, and their regular co-occurrence. Adult native speakers have a good intuitive knowledge of typical collocations; computers scanning huge amounts of text can confirm and augment those intuitions, or can make explicit what we use automatically in our everyday language. Collocating pairs of words, where the relationship is very strong and highly predictable, can thus be treated as another type of entry in our expanded lexicon. From our competence developed over a long time, and perhaps adding computer-based observations of large amounts of such data, we might arrive at a dictionary entry for 'application' that includes the following information:

application: (collocates) *submit*; *approve*; *reject*; *succeed*

The *BBI Combinatory Dictionary of English* (Benson, Benson, and Ilson 1986) attempts to organize just such information (see **10.1**).

► ## TASK 10

In the short text below, pick out typical collocations of the noun 'phone' which might form part of its entry in a dictionary, and also any unusual or marked collocations that the writer is using creatively.

'He went into a cafe and asked if he could use the phone. He dialled Sandra's number and waited. Any second now, two hundred miles away, in Sandra's flat, her phone, perched on its little mahogany table, would ring with, he hoped, a tone of urgency reflecting his panic. But would she answer it? Or, worse still, had she disconnected it, as she sometimes did when she was working? After what seemed like an eternity it purred into life and began its regulated chirping.'

Collocation also enables us to identify multi-word items and further justifies their treatment as single items of the vocabulary. The statement 'that rings a bell' (in the sense of faintly remembering something) will have its own set of collocates (name, face, number, etc.) independent of the elements that comprise the phrase.

2.2 Sense relations

Collocation is a relationship observable between items when they are arranged in texts, spoken or written. But every time we use a vocabulary item, we choose it rather than any other, and so another kind of relationship exists between items: how they are related to one another in terms of their meaning; how similar or how different they are to one another; how they may or may not substitute for one another, and so on. We can illustrate this with the following example:

| The | plan
application
scheme
proposal | was | rejected
approved
submitted
accepted | by the committee. |

A collocational relationship exists between the items in one box and the items in the other; it is a *syntagmatic* or left-to-right textual relationship.

But there are also relations between items within each box. We might feel, for instance that 'approve' and 'accept' are quite close in meaning, but opposite in meaning to 'reject', or that 'scheme' and 'plan' are quite similar, and so on. These are *paradigmatic* relations, that is, relations between different words that *might* have been chosen on the 'vertical' axis, and it is this type of relationship we shall consider now. They are often called *sense* relations to distinguish the meaning of individual items in terms of what they mean in the real world (their *denotation*) from their meaning in relation to other words within the vocabulary system of the language (their *sense*).

Both kinds of meaning are important in learning vocabulary. It is not only relevant that 'table' means a physical object in the real world, but that the word 'table' can be systematically related to the words 'chair', 'sofa', 'desk', and 'furniture' in the language system. It is to this second kind of relationship we now turn.

The relations which most language teachers encounter with the greatest frequency in day-to-day teaching are *synonymy*, *antonymy*, and *hyponymy*. These are respectively relations of sameness, oppositeness, and inclusion. None of them is a simple matter and all three are worth detailed study since they are so fundamental to the lexical organization of languages.

Synonymy

Synonymy means that two or more words have the same meaning. Many words in English appear very close in meaning to each other. 'Begin' and 'start'; 'sofa' and 'settee'; 'below', 'beneath', and 'under(neath)'; 'toilet' and 'lavatory'; 'beer' and 'ale'; 'difficulty' and 'problem', and 'adore' and 'worship' are just a few of the many hundreds of words that seem to be frequently interchangeable without loss of meaning. But are they true synonyms in that they always mean the same and can always be substituted for one another? In fact, are *any* two words ever truly synonymous in a language? All the evidence suggests that it would be unwise to declare any two items to be exact synonyms. Among factors which may distinguish words are (see Collinson 1939):

1 Two words may be close in meaning and yet not *collocate* with the same items. Native speakers of English would accept A, but not B or C:

A The baby began/started to cry as soon as they had left.
B *I couldn't begin my car; the battery was flat.
C *Before the world started, only God existed.

2 Words may have different *syntactic* behaviour. 'Leave' and 'depart' may refer to the same event but with different syntactic restrictions:

A The plane leaves/departs from Gatwick, not Heathrow.
B We left the house at six.
C *We departed the house at six.

3 Words may belong to different contexts and situations. We are here concerned with distinctions such as technical/non-technical, speech/writing, formal/informal, etc.

4 Words may be separated by geographical distribution. British people use 'lifts', Americans use 'elevators'.

5 Some words may be more archaic than others, and in the process of dropping out of the language, for example 'wireless' and 'aerodrome' have been superseded by 'radio' and 'airport' in modern English.

This type of evidence suggests that synonymy in an absolute sense has no validity in vocabulary study, and yet there is no doubt that it has great psychological validity for the majority of language learners, and provided that factors such as 1 to 5 are taken into account, learning and storing words as out-of-context synonyms could be a useful organizing principle. Dictionaries of synonyms exist, and thesauruses group words very close in meaning to one another (see **10.1**).

▶ ## TASK 11

Are the following pairs of items exact synonyms which can be interchanged in all contexts? If possible, create example sentences where the words *cannot* be interchanged.

hurry/hasten	*injure/damage*
consider/regard	*spud/potato*
pavement/sidewalk	*confess/admit*
exit/way out	

Antonymy

Antonymy, or oppositeness, may be of several kinds. In normal, everyday language, I am either 'alive' or 'dead': except in specialist medical terminology there are no intermediate terms; such opposites are normally thought of as *ungradable*. 'Hot' and 'cold' are also opposites, but there are degrees in between—'tepid', 'warm', 'cool', etc.—and terms beyond the two extremes—'scorching', 'boiling', 'freezing', etc. Opposites like 'hot' and 'cold' are therefore called *gradable*. The learner will ideally store the whole graded series for a given pair together (e.g. 'minute', 'tiny', 'small', 'little', 'average', 'medium', 'big/large', 'huge', 'enormous', etc.) but will recognize pairs like 'hot' and 'cold' as the *core* items in the series (see **4.1**; see also Carter 1987). Such series as the 'hot/cold' and 'big/small' ones are notoriously difficult to translate directly language to language: the Swedish word '*varm*' seems to have a wider range of collocates than English 'warm' and may include things that in English would be described as 'hot' (e.g. '*varmkorv*' = 'hot sausage'). Spanish '*caliente*' also seems to overlap with English 'warm' and 'hot'.

Another systematic feature of opposites is the way that one term in a pair may operate as the *unmarked* or *neutral* form. If I ask the question 'How big is your flat?' I am not presupposing that it *is* big; it may be quite small. 'Big' is neutral for size in this usage. If I ask 'How small is your flat?' then you have already told me, or I have good reason to believe that it *is* small. 'How long is *x*?', 'How wide is *x*?', and 'How high is *x*?' can all be used in this unmarked way. Such questions as these are normally learnt as idiomatic expressions by learners, but this may just be a matter of differences of realization. The underlying notion of unmarkedness is probably universal (e.g. Italian has '*Quanto* spesso *chi vai*?' = 'How *often* do you go?'; the answer may be 'Seldom').

One thing language learners will have to be aware of is that a word may have different opposites in different contexts. Consider some opposites of 'light' and 'rough' in English:

light bag	heavy bag
light wind	strong wind
light colours	dark colours
rough sea	calm sea
rough texture	smooth texture
rough area	quiet area
rough person	gentle person
rough calculation	precise calculation

▶ TASK 12

What are the possible opposites of the words 'hard' and 'high' in these phrases? Which has the most contextual variation?

high marks	hard exam
high opinion	hard chair
high building	hard journey
high price	hard work
high temperature	hard person
high winds	hard drugs

This aspect of meaning is closely related to questions of homonymy and polysemy (see **2.4**). The facts about 'light' and 'rough' presented here can also be explained in terms of collocation; the teacher will need to decide what is the clearest, most usable explanation to help the learner grasp these facts. It may be that learning collocation in terms of contextual opposites as with our 'light' and 'rough' examples will facilitate learning more than simply saying, for example, 'calm does not collocate with texture'. However, categories such as *antonymy*, *polysemy*, and *collocation*, which are of considerable use to the linguist, may not necessarily be as useful to the learner.

Hyponymy

Hyponymy, the relationship of inclusion, organizes words into *taxonomies*, or hierarchical tree-type diagrams. Consider a common word like 'car':

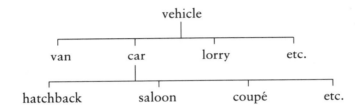

Figure 1

'Vehicle' could have been further divided into 'motor vehicles' and 'horse-drawn vehicles', with 'cart', 'carriage', and 'stagecoach' coming under the latter type. Other divisions on the basis of 'type of *x*' are also possible, for example passenger-carrying vehicles versus cargo-carrying ones. We could go further up the hierarchy and note that a vehicle is just one 'mode of transport', with 'aircraft' and 'ships/boats' forming another type. *Roget's Thesaurus* (Kirkpatrick 1987) attempts to organize the whole of the English language in this way.

In the hyponymy relation, 'car' is said to be a *hyponym* of 'vehicle', while 'vehicle' is the *superordinate* term. 'Car', 'van', and 'lorry', on the same level in the taxonomy, are called *co-hyponyms*. The whole list of co-hyponyms ('car', 'van', 'lorry', 'bus', 'motorcycle', etc.) is called a *lexical set*. The larger groupings, such as all the words under the headings of 'modes of transport' are usually called *lexical fields* (see Lehrer 1974).

Hyponymy offers another organizing principle for vocabulary teaching and learning. Most language coursebooks use this feature of organization implicitly or explicitly, in grouping names of flowers together, or garments, or articles of furniture. Taxonomies will often overlap with those of the learner's L1, but there may be misalignments too, of which teachers and materials writers would do well to be aware. The word *'hus'* in the Scandinavian languages can be used not only for a 'house' in the British sense, but more broadly too, to mean a 'building' (as in 'farm/office buildings'), which in English is the superordinate of 'house'. Taxonomies may subdivide into greater specificity in some languages than in others. The task of the learner is to map L2 taxonomies on to L1 and, ideally, note overlaps, gaps, and partial correspondences. It is worth mentioning that native-speakers themselves often do not agree on hyponymic relations: many native speakers would include 'planes' and 'boats' under the superordinate 'vehicle', while many think of 'vehicle' only in terms of 'wheeled conveyances'.

To a semanticist, the only true hyponymy is the taxonomy expressing the 'x is a *type* of y' relationship, as in 'a rose is a *type* of flower' (see Cruse 1986). But languages have other taxonomy-like relationships between words, as in these examples:

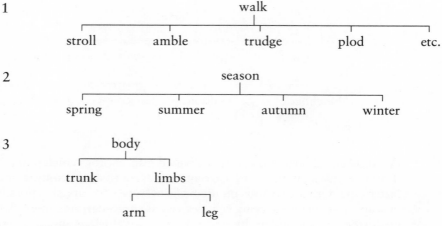

Figure 2

Number 1 is best expressed as '*ways* of doing x'; 2 is an ordered series (cf. names of months), while 3 is an 'x is *part of*' relation, sometimes called *meronymy* (see Chaffin, Herrman, and Winston 1988). Language teaching will, of course, wherever possible, take advantage of these kinds of relations too. Even in these ordered series there may be surprising mismatches between languages. For example, the 'morning', 'afternoon', 'evening', and 'night' series in English does not match one-to-one with the usual Spanish division of the day (i.e. '*mañana*', '*tarde*', '*noche*').

Whatever mismatches there may be in realizations, the organizing *principles* are universal, and taxonomy-like relations will be found in all languages; thus language teaching might hope to encourage transfer of knowledge of patterns of organization to the L2 learning context. In **3.2** we shall look at psycholinguistic evidence that language-users store words in part according to the sense relations I have described, and that presentation of semantically-related items can assist learning and retention.

▶ ## TASK 13

Construct hyponymy-trees like the one for 'car' on page 19 for the following words. What are the most general words that you have included? What are the most specific? Are there any problems?

tomato   hammer   bench

2.3 Semantic fields

In discussing hyponymy, we suggested that family tree relationships could be extended downward to words of greater specificity and upward to encompass large lexical 'fields' such as 'transport', or even larger ones such as 'motion'. The logical extension of this is to see the whole of a language as a multiplicity of lexical fields consisting of related words. These *lexical fields* are the *realization* (or flesh and bones, as it were) of the abstract notion of *semantic fields* (see Miller 1978). Semantic fields contain only concepts; lexical fields contain real words. Semantic fields are divisions within the general 'semantic space' that is available to languages to express reality, to 'word the world'. The related words and multi-word units in any given lexical field in any given language show us how that language has divided up the semantic space. A simple example would be the semantic notion of reference to proximity and distance to the speaker. English divides the space up into things the speaker considers near and immediate and those considered distant and remote. The lexical representation of this division is 'this' and 'that' and their plurals. Spanish divides the space up differently: things that are near (*este*), not so near but not remote (*ese*), and remote (*aquel*). It is often only when we look at other languages that we realize how arbitrary (or even idiosyncratic) our own language is in the way our vocabulary represents divisions of the semantic space. English conceives of 'doing' and 'making' as two distinct semantic domains regularly differentiated in such utterances as 'God made (*did) the world' and 'I've a lot of work to do (*make)' (cf. also 'she makes a lot of work for me'/'she does a lot of work for me'). Many other languages seem to subsume 'doing' and 'making' under some general notion of 'causing things to happen' (cf. Spanish '*hacer*', French '*faire*', Danish '*gøre*'. These differences within semantic fields are widespread between languages; common areas where overlap is often incomplete are verbs of cognition (i.e. knowing, thinking), spatial and temporal divisions, colour systems, kinship systems, taxonomic classifications of natural phenomena (e.g. weather, names of flora and fauna), and topographical features (e.g. words for hills, mountains, forests, etc.). In constructing the hyponymy-trees for 'tomato', 'hammer', and 'bench' in Task 13 you were reflecting on how English divides up the semantic space in the fields of 'vegetables', 'tools', and 'seating', respectively. It is by no means certain that speakers of other languages would produce identical trees for the three words in their own languages. Thus the task of the learner is to match the semantic fields of L1 and L2. What may be difficult for a learner to grasp, conceptually, is a word that realizes a semantic notion in L2 which is realized by more than one word in his or her L1, or that is perhaps not realized at all, or which is only realizable through complex paraphrase in L1.

▶ TASK 14

List as many verbs as you can think of in English for the semantic notion of 'laugh' (e.g. 'giggle', 'chuckle'); then try and translate these into another language (use a bilingual dictionary if necessary). Does the other language seem to offer more/fewer words for the overall field, and to what extent are there one-to-one correspondences? For further practice, do the same with these semantic notions:

— ways of running (e.g. 'trot', 'jog')
— words for describing the temperature of liquids

2.4 Homonymy and polysemy

Homonymy and *polysemy* are two terms used as different explanations for the fact that many word-forms in a language like English seem to occur in different contexts with quite different meanings. 'Bank' is one such example:

1 I'm just off to the *bank* to deposit a cheque.
2 The *bank* was steep and overgrown.
3 I know I can *bank* on her.

We can separate off 3 by saying that this occurrence of 'bank' is always in the form of a multi-word verb with 'on', but 1 and 2 are more problematic. The simplest explanation might be to say that 'bank' in 1 and 'bank' in 2 are homonyms, that is, words with the same *form* but different *meanings*. The learner, like the native speaker, would not necessarily associate the word 'bank' in 1 when it occurs, with the word 'bank' in 2, and would store the two words, as it were, in two different compartments, one that has collocations with 'cheque', 'deposit', 'manager', etc., and the other with 'river', 'water', 'earth', etc. Other examples of this kind in English would be:

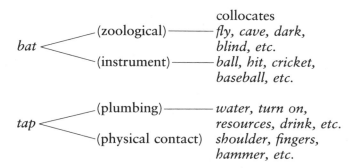

Figure 3

Many other words, though, do not lend themselves to such clear separation. Take the words 'foot' and 'head', for example:

They met at the *foot* of the mountain.
He hurt his *foot.*
There's a diagram at the *foot* of the page.

She's *head* of the department.
I'll meet you at the *head* of the valley.
Have you hurt your *head?*

'Foot' and 'head' seem to have something about their meanings that carries over from one example to the next. We feel instinctively that they are closer to one another than, say, the different meanings of 'bat' and 'tap'. Some linguists would argue that words like 'head' and 'foot' are polysemous, i.e. that 'head' is a single lexical item with multiple senses, each of which is part of the meaning potential of the word but only one of which will (usually) be actually realized in any particular context. If we take the polysemous view, there is no necessary implication that any one sense is primary: several of the senses might well be of equal importance in the mind of the language-learner or teacher. For example, the word 'catch' seems to have several related but distinct senses in English: I can catch 'a bus', 'a cold', 'a butterfly', 'someone's remarks', or 'somebody stealing money', among other things. Semantic analysis alone will not be sufficient to determine which of these senses is most basic; frequency, usefulness, psychological relevance, and many other factors may influence decisions concerning what needs to be learnt and when. Not least, the teacher will need to consider whether acquisition will be facilitated or hampered by teaching several senses of 'catch' at one go, or vice-versa, dealing with each individual sense as it crops up.

▶ **TASK 15**

Consider the following English words and decide whether they are best thought of in terms of homonymy or polysemy, and why. Try translating them into any other language you know; are there several possible translation equivalents or will one word do for the different meanings the English word has?

cap	*face*	*row* (pron. /rəʊ/)	*club*
way	*bed*	*match*	*plot*

Homonymy and polysemy would seem to be two competing labels for the description of words with more than one meaning. This conflict of labels can sometimes be resolved by looking at the historical development of words (e.g. 'ear' meaning 'human organ' and 'ear' in 'ear of corn' come from two different historical roots in English—see Palmer 1981:102). However, there are also examples in etymology of just the opposite: words from the *same* historical root but nowadays perceived as quite different words, for example, 'flower' and 'flour'. This proves that etymology may only further confuse the issue. Many language learners may not feel motivated to explore etymology and it is questionable whether such knowledge would assist acquisition (presentation of such knowledge is, to say the least, time-consuming). For most language teaching and learning purposes, the polysemy–homonymy debate will be somewhat irrelevant and the task will remain unchanged, that is, how to grapple with the variability of meaning possessed by thousands of words, not just our prime examples such as 'bank' and 'tap'. Furthermore, the problem does not end with working out a given sense of a word on a particular occasion; other questions arise, such as how is new information about a polysemous word integrated into prior knowledge of the word, and when can a learner be said to *know* a polysemous item such as 'catch'?

▶ # TASK 16

How many meanings or senses do you know for the following English words? Do some senses seem more basic or central than others? If so, which ones, and why?

top　page　button　ring

People often feel that some sense or senses of a word are in an important way basic or central, and that other senses are peripheral or unusual. Apart from the obvious (and not to be discounted) statement that the most *frequent* senses may be perceived as the most central, a statement not without its problems, two other ways of looking at central and peripheral senses may be helpful: the notion of *central or focal meaning* and the notion of *metaphorical extension*.

Central or focal meaning

In English, 'table' can mean the piece of furniture used for eating at, an ordered list of facts, or a flat area of rock or stone. For most people, the psychologically central or focal meaning is probably the first, the piece of furniture. 'Foot' in English can be a part of the body, the base of something, or a measurement; again, the first meaning is central for most speakers. Such psychological perceptions are powerful and may not necessarily coincide with actual frequency of occurrence in language data, but the power of the central meaning and its transferability across languages may be important features in how words are learnt and how different senses are felt to relate to the centre or periphery of a word's meaning potential.

▶ # TASK 17

Which would you consider to be central and peripheral senses of these English words? Arrange the senses in order of centrality, then compare your list with someone else's.

head:
1 Did you hurt your head?
2 She's head of the committee.
3 The head of this hammer is loose.

hand:
1 The hands of the clock were approaching midnight.
2 His hand was good: three kings and two aces.
3 What beautiful hands you have.
4 I need a hand; can you lift this?

You may have found that your lists agree with other people's on the question of the most central or focal meaning, but that there is variation in how people judge the relative importance of the more peripheral meanings; this is to be expected, since the peripheries of conceptual categories are usually fuzzy and not sharply delimited. You may also have found that you were processing the meanings of the peripheral senses in terms of *metaphors* based on the central or focal meanings. Your ability to do this is a fundamental part of linguistic competence and a skill that one hopes would be transferred to the processing of words in an L2.

Metaphorical extension
The central or focal meaning may often be the basis of metaphorical extensions of a word. If we see 'head' as prototypically the topmost part of a human body, then 'head of the committee/queue/valley' can carry over the feature 'topmost part of' to these other uses of 'head'. Metaphor is a way of enabling us to talk of one thing in terms of another (see 2.5). Thus 'hand' becomes a metaphor for 'help/assistance' in 'give me a hand' or 'farm-hand/factory-hand'. We might consider 'face' in the 'face of a clock' or miners working at the 'coal-face' or teachers at the 'chalk-face' to be metaphorical extensions of the human 'face'. This view of polysemy is creative; it leaves open the possibility of new metaphorical extensions of the central meaning.

The problem for the language learner is that different languages will have different degrees of polysemy attached to cognate words. Thus we should not expect the many senses of English polysemous words to be equally translatable into other languages. In English, people have 'legs' and, by metaphorical extension, so do tables; in Spanish, humans have '*piernas*', tables have '*patas*' (this latter being the word for the legs of non-human animals). Language learners are not insensitive to these problems of transferability. Kellerman (1986) has shown that Dutch students, when tested, showed such a sensitivity in judgements of translatability of the Dutch word '*oog*' (English 'eye') in its various metaphorical extensions. Kellerman's examples were:

het menselijk oog	(human eye)
het oog van een aardappel	(eye of a potato)
een electronisch oog	(electronic eye)
de ogen op een pauwestaart	(eye on a peacock's tail)
het oog van een naald	(eye of a needle)
de ogen op een dobbelsteen	(spots on a dice)

There was an overwhelming agreement that the 'human eye' would be translatable, and a very strong feeling that 'eye of a needle' and 'electronic eye' would also be translatable as 'eye' in English. Far less certainty prevailed as regards 'eyes' of a potato and on dice. Kellerman's experiment shows nicely two things: that his subjects had a clear feeling that 'human eye' was the core or prototypical meaning of '*oog*' and that the most peripheral meanings of '*oog*' would be least readily translatable by English 'eye'. Such natural instincts that learners have about vocabulary can be exploited in language learning situations. Polysemy is not a fringe aspect of language; it is at the very heart of word meaning and affects the vast majority of words, with the exception only, perhaps, of highly restricted technical terms within specialist registers, where scientific communities may agree on a single, shared meaning for a term, in which case we have a *monosemous* word.

▶ # TASK 18

Do what Kellerman's subjects did and consider the likely translatability of the English word 'back' into another language that you know. Which of the sentences could be translated using the L2 word meaning the rear part of the human body? How many different words do you think will be needed to cover the various senses of 'back'? Check your list in a good bilingual dictionary if possible.

She sat at the back of the class.
My back aches from all that work.
The index is in the back of the book.
I'm tired, I want to go back.
The back of the chair is broken.
The back of your jacket is stained.
Open the back of the camera to put the film in.

2.5 Metaphor

In **2.4**, we looked at metaphorical extensions of words like 'head' and 'eye'. Metaphor, as a device for creating and extending meaning, is very important in the study of vocabulary. Two writers on the subject, Lakoff and Johnson (1980) argue that metaphor is all-pervasive in language, and that whole cognitive domains can be the subject of metaphor. For example, if we take the metaphor ARGUMENT IS WAR, English offers a range of conventional metaphors to verbalize features of arguments:

He *made a vicious attack on my position.*
My *defences were down.*
She won't *retreat from her position.*
They *bombarded* me with objections.
I *came under fire* from all directions.

The range is not unlimited; the following sound odd as metaphors for argument:

He *shelled* my statements about the economy.
I was *bombed* by her views on education.

The fact is of crucial importance in understanding institutionalized or conventional metaphor. A fixed range of lexical items from the 'war' field is conventionally available; the fact that such a conventionally limited range is used time and time again suggests that language users are probably not even aware of the 'metaphorical' use of the lexical field any more than they are aware of the extended use of 'foot' in 'foot of the stairs' as being a metaphor. It is *un*institutionalized metaphor that stands out for the native speaker.

Many features of day-to-day life are constantly expressed metaphorically, for example, LOVE IS MADNESS:

I'm *crazy* about you.
She *drives* me *insane.*
He's *gone* all *ga-ga* since he met her.

or LOVE IS PHYSICAL UPHEAVAL:

He's *head-over-heels* in love with her.
I'm *walking on air* when I'm with him.
She makes me feel *ten feet tall.*

It will be seen that metaphor is a way of talking about one thing in terms of another. We use vocabulary from the lexical field of 'war' to verbalize semantic notions of 'argument'. We can equally well use metaphors of animal behaviour to describe people's postures and attitudes in argument, for example:

He *snapped at* her.
'I won't have it', he *barked*.
She *pounced on* his last remark.
I *fell prey* to his persuasiveness.

Such metaphors are conventional and should be treated, like other multi-word units (see **1.3**), as items in the lexicon. All languages seem to have them. They tend to operate not just as single words or items from particular fields, but as whole large sections of fields that can be transferred to another domain. Thus, in the lexical field of 'animal noises', 'bark', 'snarl', 'growl', 'purr', 'bellow', 'screech', and 'roar' are all conventionally used as metaphors for features of human speech in English. Temperature is used as a metaphor for degrees of friendliness: a person may be 'cold' or 'cool' towards another, or may be considered to have a 'warm' personality.

► TASK 19

The metaphor ARGUMENT IS WAR has produced several conventional phrases in English (see above). What words/phrases do you associate with these metaphors in English?

LIFE IS A JOURNEY/MOVEMENT THROUGH SPACE (e.g. 'She's reached the end of the road.')
EMOTION IS A PHYSICAL EXPERIENCE (e.g. 'My heart aches for him.')

Saying that metaphor enables us to talk about one thing in terms of another raises two fundamental questions: *why* we should want or need to talk about something as if it were something else, and *how* it is that the process works, that is, how speakers and listeners understand one another.

Low (1988) offers some possible answers to the first question. Low suggests that, among other things, metaphor makes it possible to conceptualize and talk about entities with vague and indeterminate boundaries, or which are abstract (e.g. how musical pitch is given *spatial* dimensions: 'high'/'low'). Metaphor may also be a way of demonstrating relations and systematicity in the real world, relations that may not be immediately obvious. Metaphor is also useful in expanding existing concepts and creating new ones (e.g. talking about the brain as though it were a computer, or about language acquisition in humans as though it were like computer-processes: 'input'/'storage'/'retrieval'/'database', etc.). Thus we can appreciate the centrality of metaphor to the encoding and decoding of language. Metaphor also seems to be connected with certain interpersonal functions such as euphemism, indirectness, evasion, and face-saving.

▶ ## TASK 20

Suggest some possible interpretations for these metaphors:

Alcoholism is *a juggernaut with a learner driver.*
The government has *microwaved, rather than cooked up,* its new economic policy.
The new proposal *is a hot coal on the carpet* of our education system.

In doing Task 20, you probably thought of features of alcoholism and juggernauts that could be related. Among features connected with alcoholism might be 'shame', 'uncontrollability', 'slow but unstoppable progress', and 'financial disaster'. 'Juggernauts' may evoke 'enormous size', 'loudness', 'uncontrollability' (if driven by a learner), 'unstoppable progress', and 'glamour'. You may have decided that the best interpretation of the metaphor was that alcoholism can be thought of in terms of some of the worst features of a learner driving a juggernaut (namely uncontrollability) and of the juggernaut itself (its slow but inevitable progress). You probably did not linger on the features of 'shame', 'pollution', and 'glamour', since they seem less relevant to constructing a link between the compared entities. The meaning of the metaphor was not just 'lying there', so to speak; *you constructed it,* by analogy, from your *linguistic* knowledge of the words involved (their semantic features and associations) and from *pragmatic* clues (you may have tried to contextualize the sentence as, for example, a doctor warning on the *dangers* of alcoholism.

This process of *construction* of meaning is a reasonable answer to the question *how* we understand metaphor. The examples in Task 20 particularly emphasize this *constructed* or *emergent* type of meaning since they are, to the best of my knowledge, not conventional metaphors but ones created, by me, as I wrote. Native speakers have, as part of their lexical competence, the ability to recognize conventional and unconventional metaphors and to understand or construct possible interpretations of both. Tolerance limits are crucial, and shift from context ·to context. Literary text tolerates far more unconventional metaphor than technical text. You may wish to test your own powers of interpretation and tolerance on randomly created metaphors such as:

I was *standing on the lampshade of* a new relationship with her.
He simply *toothached* all our proposals.

Neither is conventional, and considerable mental acrobatics are involved in any attempt at coherent interpretation.

The learner of an L2, therefore, has the following challenges to meet with regard to metaphor:

1 recognizing metaphors
2 delimiting their boundaries in text
3 distinguishing conventional and creative metaphors
4 identifying relevant or prominent features of the entities compared in order to get at an interpretation.

This can be quite difficult. Qun (1988) reports that one of the biggest difficulties for Chinese learners of English when reading the British press is the *culture-bound* features of metaphors occurring in journalism. She gives an example of the televising of the British Parliament being referred to as a 'Punch and Judy Show'. The reader would need knowledge of this highly conventionalized performance (with its quarrelsome husband and wife, its absurdities, its appeal to children, and its frivolity) to interpret the metaphor.

► TASK 21

In this news report of the beginning of a legal inquest into the deaths of three terrorists (Farrell, Savage, and McCann), metaphors are used. Identify them and consider an interpretation for them. Note any that may cause particular problems in terms of cultural knowledge.

NOW we are gathered here, hundreds of us, to report on the deliberations into the deaths of Farrell, Savage and McCann.

After only four days and eleven witnesses, it is too early to say if the circumstances of their killing will eventually join a Polish general and a Victorian sailing ship high in the league table of the unknowable. But at least the outline of a new spectral barque is showing up through the legal mists. This is the government's case.

At present only the sails and rigging are visible, in the shape of court-room curtains and radio aerials. The hull may yet prove remarkably sound and smooth. There are already signs, however, of incipient unseaworthiness.

(*Observer*, 11 September 1988)

2.6 Componential analysis

We can observe that words which cluster together to form lexical fields have certain features or attributes in common. Thus 'spaniels', 'terriers', and 'pekinese' not only have in common that they are domesticated pets, but that they are canine ones (separating them from cats). But cats and dogs *share* the attribute of being mammals, of being non-human ones, of being animate (unlike 'hammers' or 'benches') and so on. These features or attributes enable us to organize our field in terms of what the entities within it have *in common* and what *distinguishes* them from one another. A 'spaniel' and a 'terrier' have in common that they are domesticated and canine; we can express these as *semantic markers* (Katz and Fodor 1963; Carter and McCarthy 1988:30–2), and enclose the attributes in round brackets:

spaniel
terrier } (+ domesticated + canine)

Both also have in common their use as sporting or hunting dogs, and other possible features, but they also have distinguishing features, which may be expressed in square brackets (the plus signs simply mean '*possesses* that feature'):

spaniel [+ large, droopy ears + silky coat + sporting retriever]
terrier [+ small + hairy + burrowing when hunting]

The markers and distinguishing features put together are an analysis of the meaning of the word. This technique is usually called *componential analysis* (CA). The individual labels such as '+ canine' and '+ hairy' are the components of the meaning of the word. CA attempts to describe the systematic ways in which words are alike or unalike.

▶ TASK 22

Try and do the same with the following pairs of words as was done with 'spaniel' and 'terrier' above, that is, do a componential analysis illustrating the features the words in the pairs have in common (their markers) and the features that distinguish them. If possible, compare your analyses with someone else's.

hammer/mallet   *depressed/disappointed*
chicken/duck   *wallet/purse*

As an aspect of the study of vocabulary, CA is not without its problems. You may have found your analyses different from other people's, or you may have found it difficult to put into words just precisely what distinguishes a 'wallet' from a 'purse'. If you are an experienced language teacher you will be well aware of the problems of distinguishing words which, for learners, may seem to denote the same thing ('do' and 'make' are classic examples in English, as are 'say' and 'tell'). You will be equally aware that some words are difficult to describe *in words*, which is, in the end, what CA does, even though a theoretical semanticist would argue that '+ human' or '+ hairy' are just labels for semantic features, not real words at all. What are the components of meaning of 'red', or of 'wait'? Such analyses are, to say the least, very demanding, and we may feel that, for many words, meaning is best approached through analogy ('red' = 'the colour of blood'), or collocation ('wait' + 'for' + 'bus'/'train'), or a variety of other ways.

CA tends to present a rather static, abstract view of the vocabulary of a language. It is also sometimes difficult to state precisely what the components of a given word are, and subjective judgements vary. This is because our lexical competence is highly variable, is dynamic, in constant change and development. What *I* know about a word (or need to know to function socially) may not be the same as what you know. What is more, meaning changes over time and develops, and what an individual knows about a word changes too. When the language learner encounters a new word, certain features may be more salient than others; in a particular context it may be irrelevant that terriers have a burrowing instinct, in another context it might be crucial. CA does not claim to address these issues; it is more concerned with the structure of the lexicon (for further discussion see Leech 1981:117–19; see also Nida 1975). However, CA has influenced vocabulary teaching and learning, as we shall see in 7.2.

▶ ## TASK 23

Consider what features of the meaning of the following pairs of words (their common features and distinguishing features) you readily know without having to turn to a dictionary. To what extent, and to whom, might a full CA of the words be useful?

falcon/hawk   *copse/spinney*
polythene/polyurethane   *sybaritic/hedonistic*

In Task 23, you might have known that a 'falcon' and a 'hawk' are both birds of prey. You may not know whether one of the words is more general than the other or whether they are just two different varieties of the same species, and therefore may not have been able to list distinguishing features. Nor may such distinctions be important to you. To an ornithologist, however, the distinctions may be very important indeed, as may the differences between polythene and polyurethane to a scientist or building engineer.

In **2** we have sought to illustrate how linguists have attempted to describe vocabulary in terms of systematic relations between items. But how systematically, if at all, are words stored in the human mind? How organized or otherwise is our knowledge of vocabulary, and do linguists' categories of lexical relations have any psycholinguistic reality in the mind? In **3** we shall consider these questions under the title of the *mental lexicon*.

3 The mental lexicon

3.1 Introduction

In any discussion of language and the mind, it should never be forgotten that our knowledge is relatively scant and that at best we can only create partial models, speculating and using metaphors borrowed from things we *do* understand considerably better, such as dictionaries, encyclopaedias, libraries, or computers. But we can observe features of language development and general linguistic behaviour that offer us glimpses as to how the mind might possibly cope with something as vast as the vocabulary of a language. After all, educated adult speakers have knowledge of tens, possibly even hundreds of thousands, of words of their language (Aitchison 1987:5–7) and can summon up the appropriate word in milliseconds. This has led researchers to believe that the mind must *organize* words in some way. What we should not necessarily assume is that the mind organizes the lexicon of a second language in the same way as it does its first, nor that the processes of comprehension and production necessarily operate on the same mental bases (Channell 1988).

▶ **TASK 24**

Consider briefly and, if possible, discuss with someone, what broad implications the following metaphors have for the study of the mental lexicon. Are there any other metaphors you find appealing?

The mental lexicon is
$\left\{\begin{array}{l}\text{a dictionary} \\ \text{a thesaurus} \\ \text{an encyclopaedia} \\ \text{a library} \\ \text{a computer}\end{array}\right.$

3.2 Input, storage, and retrieval

Whichever metaphor of those listed you found most attractive, you may have noticed they all had in common the idea of *input* (i.e. that language is 'written in' in some way), *storage* (that it is held and not lost), and *retrieval* (that it can be 'called up' when needed for use). The dictionary metaphor, for instance, implies the notion that a word and its meanings are 'written in' together (along with its spelling and, possibly, information about word-class, pronunciation, etymology, and derivations), that this information is stored as an alphabetical list, perhaps with some cross-referencing, and can be searched quickly and economically for the meaning of a given form. The thesaurus metaphor is slightly different; here we presuppose a meaning, for which the thesaurus, classified into semantic fields, can provide us with a selection of closely related words from which we choose. The encyclo-paedia metaphor suggests that words carry with them crucial links with other types of knowledge, including historical, perceptual, and social knowledge. The computer metaphor suggests split-second processing ability, complex storing with myriad cross-referencing, and virtually instant recall. The computer also gives us the idea of dynamic input, constantly updating itself and re-sorting its data, something that diction-aries and encyclopaedias are slower to do. The library metaphor tries to capture constantly updated input and theoretically limitless storage, all under the control of cataloguers, and quick paths to the book needed. Each of these metaphors may prove useful in part to describe what we know about the mental lexicon.

Input

For children learning their mother tongue, virtually all linguistic input in their first years is spoken, that is, nothing but a stream of sounds. For the student of a second or foreign language it is likely that spoken and written language will play equally important roles right from the start. Indeed, many millions of language learners around the world have learnt, and are still learning, languages with very little spoken input at all. So words may well be perceived by L2 learners as much in terms of their *orthographic* shape as their *phonological* shape, or they may have a special storage tag which relates oddities between the two, such as silent letters in some English words, for example the orthographic patterning of *-ugh* words ('laugh', 'tough', 'though') or the *silent 'b'* words ('womb', 'lamb', 'comb'). The learner, in an ideal world, should come to recognize verbal input in a flash. How learners might achieve this is clearly not unconnected to how native-speakers do it. For native-speakers, the *general shape* of the incoming word is important, not every minute contour of its make-up. This phenomenon is sometimes known as the 'bathtub' effect, that is, that the front and rear ends of words are prominent but the middle 'dips' a bit, so to speak (see Aitchison 1987: 119–21). Speakers recognize the first and last syllables of words and take note of how many syllables they contain, the general rhythmic structure, and where the stress falls. So, in recognizing the following words, the *im___ly* structure with four syllables is important, as is the main stressed syllable:

im*med*i**ately   im***pos*sibly   im***pa*tiently   im***per*viously

When people have a word 'on the tip of their tongue', they can often say quite a lot about the word, including these features of its general shape, yet still be unable to call up the exact word.

▶ TASK 25

Test yourself on the bathtub phenomenon. How many words can you recall that fit these patterns? For example:

sa__tion (*saturation, salutation, sanitation*)
dis__ion
pro__ion
en__ment

The language learner may benefit from crucial information about the syllable structure and *citation-form* stress pattern of a word (i.e. how it is stressed out of context) in assisting the storage and memorization process. I was able to call up the words 'immediately', 'impossibly', 'impatiently', and 'imperviously' quickly and without using a dictionary even though they come from quite different semantic fields, which suggests I have a pattern of syllables and stress associated with those words. Such insights are sometimes employed directly in language teaching (see 8.2). Research shows that the 'tip of the tongue' phenomenon is similar in L1 and L2 (Channell 1988), which suggests that 'general shape' is an important feature of the mental lexicon of L1 and L2 in terms of matching input to stored patterns and in retrieving specific items from such stored templates.

The input metaphor raises two other key questions: what type of input is best, and just how much new input can the mind cope with? Language teachers could, and in many cases do, input words in the form of word-lists with various kinds of definition and explanation, or words and translation equivalents in the learner's L1, or else embed our input in contexts. All three methods work in some way, but none is without its problems. People can memorize quite long lists of words, but it is questionable whether these are retained over long periods and to what extent they assist quick recall. Translation equivalents might speed recall by providing a 'path' routed through the learner's highly efficient L1 mental lexicon, but might hinder the development of the internal organization of an efficient and separate L2 lexicon. There is also the question of the 'direction' of learning translation equivalents; does one input a pre-ordained list of L1 words and learn their L2 equivalents, or vice-versa? The answer may depend on whether comprehension or production is the more important goal for the learner (see Carter and McCarthy 1988:14). Research is frustratingly inconclusive as to whether presenting and learning words in context is superior to learning words by pairs of translation equivalents (ibid.:15), but most language teachers feel that contextualized input is vital, even from the earliest stages; arguably, learners do not get any real grasp of a word anyway until they have performed some sort of mental contextualization upon it. What is more, many other factors affect learnability for a given item (see 6.2).

▶ TASK 26

Consider any second or foreign languages you have learnt and list the predominant types of input you were subjected to. If possible, compare your list with others'. Can you come to any conclusions about the efficacy of different inputs at different stages of your learning?

So far we have considered input as a conscious matter of 'feeding' language to the subject, but, of course, learners are subjected to informal inputs too, where vocabulary may be acquired almost unconsciously. In the case of English, this may be in the form of radio and television, films, pop music, internationally marketed commercial products, and the international use of languages like English and French at airports and in other travel contexts. Little is known about precisely how much vocabulary is absorbed and acquired in this way, but all language teachers are familiar with groups of 'beginners' who already seem to have some vocabulary, and of learners on courses who learn items not in the coursebook. One challenge to vocabulary teaching is to maximize the benefits of these informal inputs.

▶ TASK 27

Make a list of English words the average young person might be expected to know before embarking on an English as a foreign language course, as a result of exposure to films, pop culture, television, international marketing, and so on. Compare your list with someone else's and see how many words emerge in total.

For me, when I first began to learn one of my foreign languages, Swedish, the films of Ingmar Bergman with English subtitles were an important source of vocabulary input, but the first few films I saw often caused me to 'switch off' as regards the soundtrack and to use only the subtitles, simply because there were just *too many* new words. So there are limits as to how many new words the mind can absorb and deal with, and there are no pat answers to the question 'how many new words per text/per hour should language learners be subjected to?' Beginners are often dealt a surprisingly heavy load of new vocabulary. If we assume the knowledge of the absolute beginner to be zero words, then in just the first unit of the *Cambridge English Course Book 1* (Swan and Walter 1984), a cascade of more than eighty new words descends on the user. Of course, not all of these are intended to be fully understood and learnt on first encounter, and some language courses make explicit at the end of each unit just which words are the ones to be learnt or focused on (e.g. *The COBUILD English Course Book 1*, Willis and Willis 1988).

But decisions do have to be made on a commonsense basis, especially in the matter of grading input such as reading texts. Nation and Coady (1988) note that L1 and L2 studies of optimal ratios of known words to unknown words in reading texts do not greatly differ. L1 research certainly shows that comprehension is impeded if one new word occurs in every three words, but the difficulties are relatively slight with one new word in every twelve. One L2 research experiment suggests that learners can handle up to one new word in every fifteen words of a 750-word text, so the differences are not enormous. Of course, much also depends on the *length* of text and the purpose of the communication. The density of assimilable new words in *spoken* input might be expected to be different too, owing to the different processing constraints.

► ## TASK 28

These lines from a poem by Lewis Carroll may give you the experience of confronting a very high density of new words in a text. What is the ratio of known to unknown words for you?

'Twas brillig, and the slithy toves
Did gyre and gimble in the wabe;
All mimsy were the borogoves,
And the mome raths outgrabe.
(Lewis Carroll: *Through the Looking-Glass*)

You may not have known many of the words in the poem, but you probably used a variety of clues to attach some sort of meaning to them, not least their position in the syntax, their morphology and lexical echoes, and the feelings and moods evoked by certain sounds. Your reactions may not be unconnected with how you store vocabulary in your mind.

Storage

Storage metaphors try to capture the essence of organization in the mental lexicon and to illustrate the ways in which individual items cross-refer to one another. Taking the dictionary metaphor, we can expect each word to have attached to it a meaning, a syntactic class, a sound pattern, a spelling pattern (especially in languages where sound and spelling often have mismatches), perhaps some derivations clustering around it and, if it is a well-organized dictionary, cross-references to synonyms and even antonyms. We have seen how 'tip-of-the-tongue' phenomena suggest that sound patterns in the form of a 'general' shape for the word seem to be in the storage system, but what about other features?

For English, native speakers do seem to store words according to spelling patterns too. Most adult native speakers could fairly quickly call up sets of words with similar spellings (e.g. words ending in '-ough'), and people will intuitively answer questions, such as 'how do you spell *honey*?' with 'like *money*' (as opposed to 'like *funny*')—something of a feat if we remind ourselves that tens of thousands of items are held in store. The L2 learner will, it is hoped, develop similar cross-references for spelling.

▶ ## TASK 29

See how quickly you can call up other English words with similar spelling patterns to these words:

pail   pale   comb   loan   phone

In Task 29, you were cross-referencing words widely different in meaning to a given orthographic pattern of a type which clearly has some (even if limited) organizing power in your mental lexicon. If I introduced you to a new word /zeɪl/ one of the things you would wish to know was whether it was written '*zail*', '*zale*', or '*zeil*', and you would automatically classify it in its appropriate family. But you would probably want to know: (a) what it meant when I used it; (b) what other meanings it has, and (c) what word class(es) it could be used in.

To say that information about meaning is stored is a truism, but it is by no means simple to capture just what it is we store. Componential analysis (see 2.6) suggested that words could be 'decomposed' into the bits that make up their meaning, but it is extremely doubtful that semantic markers have any strong psychological reality: linguists cannot seem to agree anyway what the set of primitive markers would be, and experiments suggest that words are processed instantaneously for meaning and *not* first broken down into components (see Aitchison 1987:67–9).

A slightly different matter is whether word-meanings are organized in relation to one another, and here the evidence seems to point towards strong links between words. In this respect, evidence of moment-by-moment problems in speech data offers clues to types of meaning relation. For example, people sometimes produce *blends* in their L1, where half of one word crowds in on half of another:

'It was absolutely tinute.'   *(tiny/minute)*
'It's on the dressing-board.'   *(dressing-table/sideboard)*

Synonyms and co-hyponyms seem to be competing as candidates for the right word in these examples, suggesting that the accessing mechanism has found the right 'bundles' of words but not exactly the right one (see also Channell 1988). Equally important is word-association evidence; people respond in consistent ways, even if the words they respond with are different, in word-association tests. While we should not necessarily conclude that word-association games mirror the *retrieval* process in any way, they do seem to suggest that words are organized into semantically related families in the mind. Aitchison (1987:73ff.) reports that *co-ordination* is the commonest feature of native-speaker word-association responses; words on the same level of detail will be given in responses (this includes opposites):

stimulus		response
salt	$\longrightarrow$	*pepper*
butterfly	$\longrightarrow$	*moth*
red	$\longrightarrow$	*blue*
left	$\longrightarrow$	*right*

Also frequent are *collocational* links: stimulus words give responses that collocate regularly with the stimulus:

stimulus		response
butterfly	$\longrightarrow$	*net*
bright	$\longrightarrow$	*red*
salt	$\longrightarrow$	*water*

Other associations are *superordination*, where a superordinate is given (this is particularly so where the superordinate is a frequent, readily available label), and *synonymy* (where the stimulus word produces a synonym).

▶ # TASK 30

Test yourself (and some friends if you can) by giving the first word that associates in your mind with each of these words. Then check your results against the types discussed above (co-ordination, collocation, superordination, synonymy):

grass   Monday   big   herring   sneeze   chair

If the L1 lexicon seems to associate words according to clearly definable types of relation, it may not be necessarily so for L2. Learners may for a long time lack the ability to make instantaneous collocational associations, and may be more inclined to associate L2 words by sound similarities.

▶ # TASK 31

Test yourself by writing down five words in any foreign language you know and then write beside each one the first word in that language that comes to mind. How do your results compare with L1-based association tests?

Word-association results suggest that words are organized semantically. If the thesaurus metaphor is a true reflection of mental storage, then the mind would seem to consist of bundles of related words, united into larger bundles, just like the divisions and sub-divisions of *Roget's Thesaurus*. But this is an oversimplification. Native-speakers can say a lot more about a word than just what co-ordinates, collocates, and superordinates, or what synonyms it has. My knowledge of the word 'war' brings with it associations of reading about the history of the two world wars in Europe, nuclear war, my vague memories of rationing and identity cards in Britain, and the sorts of people who use the word proudly and those who use it with condemnation. Somewhere, the word is related by an intricate series of links to an encyclopaedia of world knowledge gathered over many years. Encyclopaedic information is also organized and may often provide links between words; thus if I associate 'war' with 'gas-masks', 'ration-books', 'certain political beliefs', and 'murder' I am doing more than using semantic information. This kind of knowledge produces a web-like set of associations:

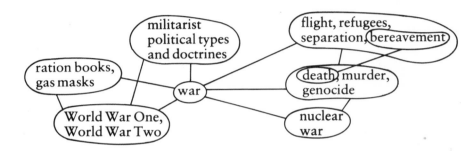

Figure 4

Each circle will, in turn, contract relations with other webs: 'flight' and 'refugees' may link with 'famine', 'drought', and words associated with the effects of such disasters. Encyclopaedic knowledge relates words to the world, and brings in origins, causes, effects, histories, and contexts.

► TASK 32

Construct an encyclopaedic web for the word 'railway' in terms of your world knowledge. Consider not only what a railway *is* but the origins, effects, contexts, etc. of 'railways'. If possible, compare your web with one constructed by somebody from a different cultural background.

The discussion of semantic relations such as hyponymy and meronymy in **2.2** modelled the vocabulary in terms of taxonomies, but this now seems to be a gross simplification compared with the complexities of how words are stored in the mind: 'webs' or 'nets' might be better metaphors for how information is attached to words in the mental store, but the total model for the place of any word in the lexicon will have to be three-dimensional, with phonological nets crossing orthographic ones and criss-crossing semantic and encyclopaedic nets. We might construct a small portion of the model (for the word 'television') as follows:

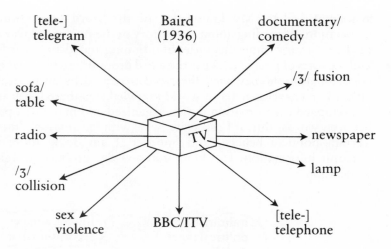

Figure 5

Each 'line' radiates out to further 'boxes' in many directions; each word in the diagram can itself be seen as a box with its own three-dimensional lines.

As long as we remember that 'webs', 'nets', 'boxes', and 'lines' are just metaphors for the complexities of the cross-referencing mechanisms in the mind, they are useful illustrations of the vastly complex nature of the mental store. Obviously, our description does not end here; additionally, word-class and other syntactic features are also part of a word's make-up and are stored in the mental lexicon. The language learner has a formidable task in emulating the complexities of L1 storage in an L2 and, naturally, the L2 mental lexicon will have to develop from a few initial strands to the goal of labyrinthine connections between words. Not least, the learner will probably be under greater stress and at a considerable disadvantage in *retrieving* items from the mental lexicon of L2, compared with the ease with which the lexicon of L1 can be consulted.

One final word about input and storage returns us to the computer and library metaphors. The mental lexicon is never static; it is constantly receiving new input which has to be integrated into the existing store. Not only do new words come in but information about existing words is added too. This is a more obvious phenomenon for the learner and the L2 lexicon, but it is also true of L1. The webs of meanings and associations constantly shift and re-adjust; new connections are woven, and old ones strengthened.

Retrieval

Our last statement above, that the mental lexicon is in constant flux, raises an awkward question: just what does it mean when we say we *know* a word, and, more particularly, when can it be said that a language learner *knows* a word in L2?

▶ TASK 33

Think of what it means for a learner to *know* a word in L2 and then complete this sentence:

'A language learner knows an L2 word when . . .'

Compare your answer with someone else's.

The relationship between *knowing* and the ability to *retrieve* that knowledge may not be direct, and we feel nothing but frustration when we have to say 'I know her name perfectly well, but I just can't think of it'. But what we know about words and what we can retrieve for practical use may not be quite the same, and will vary from word to word.

Your definition of *knowing* may have included, as well as *knowledge* (about spelling, pronunciation, meaning, etc.) something about the *ability to summon up the word* when required. In other words, if a language learner cannot actively use a particular word when it is needed, without too much mental searching, then we might feel that we are dealing with an incomplete knowledge of the word, or at the very least we shall want to distinguish between *receptive* knowledge and *productive* knowledge.

▶ TASK 34

Test your ability to 'retrieve' some less common English words that fit the definitions given below. You are given the first letter(s):

1 draw the eyebrows together in worry, puzzlement, or concentration: *f*_____
2 pad or notebook for making quick, informal notes: *j*_____
3 instrument for cutting grass: *l*_____-*m*_____
4 metal part which a belt or strap passes through in order to fasten it: *b*_____

Much of our everyday use of vocabulary is fluent and automatic; we have remarkably fast retrieval skills. *Receptive retrieval* involves matching spoken or written input to stored sound and orthographic patterns and their associated meanings. As we saw earlier, words seem to be associated with a general syllabic shape and stress pattern, and this explains why hearers can decode messages despite heavy background noise in their L1 (but compare your ability to interpret an indistinct public announcement in an L2!); it also explains why readers can read fast, without analysing every letter (and why proof-reading a typescript for spelling errors is, in fact, quite difficult). The learner may often be slowed down in the retrieval of meaning by over-concentration on word-analysis and may have to re-read or say 'please repeat/speak more slowly', even when the message contains 'known' words.

Retrieving the appropriate meaning depends on matching verbal input with features of the context and going very rapidly to the appropriate meaning. It would be highly wasteful if, every time the word 'make' occurred, the mind had to search every possible meaning of 'make' for the right one. Instead, contexts contain *anchor words* that narrow down the possible search paths so that we go direct to the meaning; anchor words are words of low semantic variability which interact with other words in the text to narrow down the meaning options (Moore and Carling 1982:196).

▶ TASK 35

Consider these sentences and note how the surrounding words progressively narrow down the options for decoding 'make'. What would be the best paraphrase of the meaning of 'make' here?

They made it.
They made it by hand.
They made it by hand out of soot and water.

• Idioms and fixed phrases are decoded as 'chunks' and not taken apart and analysed. Experimentation has shown that a phrase such as 'he was skating on thin ice' will be interpreted idiomatically by native-speaker informants rather than analysed and interpreted literally (Gibbs 1986). Fixed phrases such as 'how d'you do?' and 'by and large' have unique retrieval paths taking us straight to the meaning of the multi-word unit; in terms of the library metaphor, 'by', 'and', and 'large' each have their own individual catalogue references, and 'by and large' as a unit also has its own unique catalogue reference.

▶ TASK 36

Consider the words 'unforgettable', 'reproduce', and 'decontamin-ate'. Does it seem to you, when you hear or read these words, that you understand them as wholes, or that you have to 'take them apart' (e.g. *re* = 'again', *produce* = 'make/cause'; therefore, *reproduce* = 'make again')?

All the linguistic and experimental evidence seems to suggest that derived words (see **1.2**) such as those in Task 36 are stored separately, as *wholes* (see Aitchison 1987: 107–17) in the L1 mental lexicon. Again, 'produce' will have its own catalogue entry, so will 'reproduce', and so, indeed, will the prefix 're-', for use in creative formations and interpreting new formations not yet part of the individual store. Thus, the retrieval process goes straight to the stored derived, compounded, or phrasal form without prior analysis.

Productive retrieval follows reverse paths to those of receptive retrieval: meanings have to be given forms; some of the forms will be simple words, some will be derived words and compounds, some binomials, fixed collocations, and other multi-word units (see **1.3**). The economy in the retrieval process provided by pre-assembled chunks of these kinds is seen as a useful means whereby L2 learners can access such segments of language very quickly and from a very early stage in learning a foreign language (see Nattinger 1988). Over-concentration on learning single words may hinder the development of the L2 phrasal lexicon and deny the opportunities this gives for rapid retrieval and fluent, connected speech in the stressful conditions of speaking and writing.

The terms *receptive retrieval* and *productive retrieval* might seem at first to be jargonistic elaborations of the old *passive* versus *active* vocabulary distinction; in fact they are deliberately intended not to be so. The active/passive distinction has been under attack for some time (e.g. see Færch, Haastrup, and Phillipson 1984:99). It is rejected on the grounds that it takes a simplistic view of the way in which the lexicon is stored in the mind, i.e. as a static thing kept in two separate compartments. The computer metaphor of retrieval, with its emphasis on search processes, enables us to capture the variable procedures involved in understanding words as input and in producing words as output.

But before moving away from the computer metaphor, we need to say more about the *nature* of what is stored in the mental lexicon and, in particular, how the words therein are related to meanings in the world.

3.3 Prototypes

One of the problems researchers encounter when investigating how people perceive semantic fields is that the lexical fields that realize them do not seem to consist of an array of words of equal status. In any given field, some words will seem more salient, will spring more immediately to mind, and will be perceived as 'classic examples' of that field. This phenomenon seems to reflect the fact that some concepts are more salient or more central than others within the semantic field. For a variety of reasons, some cultural, some personal, some, it seems shared widely across speech communities, certain entities are seen as more central representatives of their class than others. Most British people, if asked to judge the 'dogginess' of different types of dog, will plump for terriers and sheepdogs as more central representatives of their class than pekinese or poodles. Terriers and sheepdogs, for British people anyway, may be considered to be *prototypes* of dogs. Shading away from them will be canine creatures more or less doggy-like until the class merges in a fuzzy boundary with hyenas, wolves, foxes, and so on.

▶ TASK 37

Look at these pictures of various vessels. Which of them seems to be the prototype of a 'cup' in English? Do any of them fall outside the idea of 'cup'?

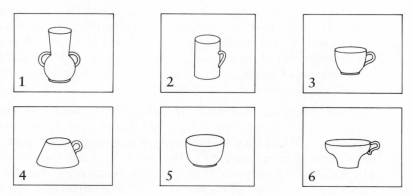

Figure 6

Labov (1973) examined the problems in establishing prototypical criteria for 'cup'. Rosch (1973) also investigated perceptions of the prototypicality of words within fields and discovered overwhelming preferences among her subjects for particular items as prototypes. Here are some examples for 'fruit', 'vehicle', and 'sport'. The lists represent a descending order of prototypicality; the first item in each list was usually preferred by a large majority of respondents:

fruit: *apple, plum, pineapple, strawberry, fig, olive*
vehicle: *car, boat, scooter, tricycle, horse, skis*
sport: *football, hockey, wrestling, archery, gymnastics, weightlifting*

▶ TASK 38

Match your own perceptions against the results reported by Rosch. Here is a jumbled list of items. Rank them in an order which represents *your* stereotype of a 'bird'.

chicken, ostrich, bat, robin, wren, eagle

Compare your list with the Rosch list on page 48.

3.4 Meaning and cognition

Prototypes raise many questions as to the type of knowledge that we store about words and their *cognitive* representations. In 2.6 we suggested that a description of word-meaning that took into account only componential features, or which only located words in semantic fields, was 'inadequate', and that much of our knowledge of words was more like the kinds of information found in encyclopaedias rather than dictionaries or thesauruses. Psycholinguists are interested in how this *encyclopaedic knowledge* is structured and how we decode and encode language in relation to it.

► ## TASK 39

Make brief notes on everything you know about *apples* (e.g. shape, taste, type of fruit, etc.). Compare your notes with other people's if possible. What common features are there among different people's conceptions and what different *types* of knowledge are they displaying?

Psycholinguists work with the notion of *cognitive domains*. A useful distinction is that between *basic* domains and *abstract* domains. Basic domains are such universal and fundamental qualities as *dimensions*, including ideas such as *time*, *pitch*, and *temperature*, whereas abstract domains are schematic representations of particular entities, for example, the idea of *body* would be the abstract domain within which we identify specific notions like *finger*, *hand*, and *arm*. Your knowledge of *apples* probably included dimensional knowledge and basic features such as *taste* and *smell*, but it may have also included features from abstract domains, such as that they are eaten, they grow on trees, and they are found in temperate climates, (see Langacker 1987:154 for a discussion of *banana* on these lines). To say everything we need to say to understand how the word 'apple' may occur in use requires specifications from different cognitive domains. Prototypes characteristically consist of clusters of features from different domains (*cup* will evoke certain features of solidity, compact size, etc. but will also involve ideas of what it is used for, for example, for drinking tea or coffee, but not typically beer) and every use of the word 'cup' *activates* these domains in the mind of the receiver. Abstract domains are also referred to as *schemata*, a term associated with *schema theory*. Schema theory essentially says that words do not hold meaning inherently, 'but only through the access they afford to different stores of knowledge that allow us to make sense of them' (Langacker 1987:155). The implication of this view is that language requires cognitive effort; it is all too easy to think that a dictionary definition or a brief explanation of a new word for a learner is sufficient for a decoding of its meaning; it has to be matched and integrated into the knowledge store and, above all, success in comprehension depends on activating the appropriate cognitive domains. The basic domains may well be universal, but schemata or abstract domains may differ from culture to culture (see Carrell and Eisterhold 1983). For example, the word 'wedding' will evoke different settings and events in different cultures.

▶ # TASK 40

Consider your prototype image of the word 'hat'. Draw a picture of it if you can. What basic and abstract domains (or schemata) are activated by the word?

If you are British, your prototype of *hat* may well be something of the kind associated with Queen Elizabeth's headgear, or else a bowler or a trilby type. But if I say 'the baby needs a hat' the abstract domain is modified to exclude those types mentioned, and the world of babies has to be activated, with its typical bonnet-type headgear. The meaning-in-context of *hat* thus *emerges*, or is *constructed*, rather than *is* the word 'hat'. This is done by a series of activations of appropriate domains (for 'emergent' theories of meaning see Moore and Carling 1982:151–63). In language teaching and learning, activating the cognitive processes that lead to comprehension will be crucial, and different words will create different types of difficulty when it comes to matching and integrating them with stored knowledge.

The cognitive processes, then, connected with the encoding and decoding of words, take us far beyond semantics and into encyclopaedic knowledge and its relationship with the pragmatics of situations in which words are used. Language use involves cognitive activity; meanings emerge from words in use and are created in the mind by elaborate acts of relating and matching different kinds of knowledge. Without such activity, we could never cope with something as central and universal in language use as metaphor.

List from Rosch (1973) for comparison in Task 38:

Category	Member	Frequency
Bird	Robin	377
	Eagle	161
	Wren	83
	Chicken	40
	Ostrich	17
	Bat	3

4 Vocabulary in use

We shall now begin to look at how we have to alter our perspectives on words the moment we start to involve the users of language in our description, and consider some of the uses to which vocabulary is put.

One of the first questions to look at is whether, in the vocabulary of a language like English, all words are of equal status or whether some words are more central to language use than others. We shall then look at how different vocabulary is employed by different users in different contexts, and how vocabulary helps to structure longer stretches of language as coherent discourse.

4.1 Core vocabulary

One way of looking at the status of words in lexical fields is to consider whether some words are more *core*, or central to the language, than others. The idea that there might be a core or basic vocabulary of words at the heart of any language is quite an appealing one to language educators, for if we could isolate that vocabulary then we could equip learners with a survival kit of core words that they could use in virtually any situation, whether spoken or written, formal or informal, or in any situation where an absolutely precise term, the *mot juste*, might be elusive and where a core word would do.

In any given lexical field, core words tend to be the most frequently occurring ones, but this may be just a circular way of saying people use such words most frequently because they do have core meaning-potential and are therefore useable in a wide variety of situations.

Carter (1987) offers examples of core words and how we might distinguish them. Consider the set of words comprising the lexical field of 'having a weight above the norm'; we have in English 'fat', 'obese', 'overweight', 'plump', 'podgy', 'stout', and several other words. We would probably guess that 'fat' was the most frequent. We can also say about 'fat' that it would normally be used to describe or define the other words, but not vice-versa. But we can also say the same about 'overweight'. 'Fat' and 'overweight' would also be likely to occur in a wider variety of contexts: 'a fat baby'/'an overweight baby' sounds far more likely than 'a stout baby'; 'fat' might further be found in the context of farm-animals, without any implication that the animals were 'overweight'. 'Fat' seems to form an immediate relationship of antonymy with 'thin'; the antonyms of 'plump' and 'podgy' are less obvious. 'Overweight' might be considered more neutral in the interpersonal sense, less likely to give offence and perhaps more clinical. On the other hand, 'obese' seems definitely to carry negative evaluation. 'Fat' seems to collocate more widely than all the others and can be more readily used metaphorically and in idioms: 'a fat wallet'/'salary'/'book', 'a fat chance', 'the fat of the land'. 'Fat' is polysemous and can be used in different word-classes: meat has 'fat' on it, we can fry food in 'fat', we have a verb 'to fatten' and so on. Therefore, applying a wide variety of tests to the words in our list seems to suggest that 'overweight' and 'fat' are more core than the rest, and that 'fat' seems to be the most core item in the set. The other words in the set will have a far narrower band of useability.

▶ TASK 41

Using tests similar to those described above, decide which are the core words in these sets. What reasons would you give?

slim, slender, thin, emaciated, scrawny
cause, bring about, effect, instigate, precipitate
scarlet, vermilion, crimson, red, ruddy

Native-speaker informants have a good instinct for which words are core words in any given field, and teachers and materials writers base many of their decisions on what to present and teach on such instincts. As always, the question of how language *learners* perceive the coreness of words is a different one and there are likely to be problems with *cognate* words (words which are similar in two languages because they are derived from the same source). Cognate words may be 'false friends' because they differ in their degree of coreness. English 'go' is more core than Swedish '*gå*', the latter meaning usually 'to go *on foot*': Swedish '*gå*', is inappropriate for English sentences such as 'I'm going to Yugoslavia next month'. We would hope that encounters with words in a wide variety of contexts would gradually build up a profile of meaning for a word and would enable the learner to relate it to its near neighbours in terms of closeness or remoteness to the core. 'Ruddy' and 'carmine' are both related to core 'red', but 'ruddy' occurs in more combinations ('face', 'cheeks', 'complexion') than 'carmine', which is very rare outside of literary usage. The learner who described someone as having a 'carmine complexion' would probably raise a laugh!

4.2 Procedural vocabulary

Identifying items in the lexicon that seem to carry a heavy work-load (e.g. the core vocabulary) must include a consideration of how some words are characteristically used to talk about other words, to paraphrase them and define them and to organize them in communication. Widdowson (1983) describes this kind of vocabulary as 'procedural'. Robinson (1988) refers to 'the simple lexis of paraphrase and explanation' to illustrate procedural vocabulary and calls the procedural words 'the main element in our interpretation and categorization of specific frames of reference'. He gives an excellent example in two dictionary entries:

---

ver·mic·u·lite /vɜːˈmɪkjʊlaɪt‖vɜrˈmɪkjə-/ *n* [U] a type of MICA that is a very light material made up of threadlike parts, that can be used for keeping heat inside buildings, growing seeds in, etc.
ver·mi·form /ˈvɜːmᵻfɔːm‖ˈvɜrmᵻfɔrm/ *adj* shaped rather like a worm

---

(*Longman Dictionary of Contemporary English* 1978)

The key vocabulary here is 'type', 'material', 'made up', 'parts', 'used', 'keep', 'shaped', and 'like'. These words, we may note, are *core words* (see **4.1**) and are higher order superordinates in *hyponym-trees* (see **2.2**); these, and many other superordinate and general words like them, are highly useful not only in *talking about* specific words like 'vermiculite' but also in the *cognitive* process of categorizing and organizing features of meaning relative to other, known entities. Thus 'vermiculite' is crucially a *material*, *made up* of *a, b, c, used* for *x, y, z*; it is a *type* of something too. All our key words in these definitions are part of the procedural vocabulary enabling us to talk about and conceptualize the relationships between items and between fields, and to locate items within fields as we acquire them.

▶ # TASK 42

Look up the definitions of 'graphite', 'hydrometer', and 'perennial' in a monolingual English dictionary and identify basic procedural vocabulary used in the definitions. You could also try looking up the equivalents of these words in another language and comparing the procedural vocabulary with that used in English.

Widdowson (1983:92) makes a distinction between words which are *schematically* bound and words of high *indexical* (or *procedural*—they are synonymous) potential. The schematically bound words narrow the frames of reference and identify particular fields; 'hydrometer' has low indexical potential and will occur in a narrow range of texts identifiable within certain scientific and technical fields. 'Instrument', however, which you may well have found figuring in the dictionary definition of 'hydrometer', has high indexical potential; it will occur in a very wide range of contexts and can be used to define, and locate within their fields, a vast number of entities. Further along what is, in fact, a continuum between the schematic and the indexical are words like 'make', 'move', and 'use', and even further, words like 'do' and 'have', merging into the so-called pure function-like words.

▶ TASK 43

Look at this extract from a text about endocrine systems. Identify
important indexical words and consider what they tell you about the
schematically bound words around them:

'The adrenal cortical hormones are steroids; i.e., compounds that,
as noted in the section on the testes (see below), contain the
cyclopentanoperhydrophenanthrene nucleus. They are conve-
niently divided on a functional basis into: (1) mineralcorticoids,
hormones that have their major action on the excretion of sodium
and potassium; (2) glucocorticoids, hormones that affect the
metabolism of glucose, other carbohydrates, and protein; and (3)
sex hormones, including both androgens and estrogens, that have
the same functions as the gonadal steroids discussed previously.'
(From 'Endocrine Systems' in *The New Encyclopaedia Britannica*,
Fifteenth edition)

The key procedural or indexical words such as 'contain', 'divided', 'affect',
'same', and so on enable me, a complete newcomer to the field of endocrine
systems, to locate hyponymic ('type of *x*') and meronymic ('part of *x*')
relations within this field and to isolate markers and distinguishing features
in a very basic componential analysis of adrenal cortical hormones. The
procedural vocabulary is crucial in my capacity to infer meanings.
Obviously, this is not enough. As Lehrer (1985) has pointed out, it is not
much use to me to know that *x* is a co-hyponym of *y* unless I can identify *x*
and *y* in the real world and locate them within some schematic frame of
reference: we need sense (relations *between words*) and denotation
(relations *between words and the world*) (see **2.2**) in conjunction.
However, learners at all levels will need to confront the procedural lexicon
of the language they are learning.

4.3 Discourse

In recent years, discourse analysis has become more and more prominent in
applied linguistics. Discourse analysts are concerned with features that
connect language with the contexts in which it is used: that is, how such
things as telephone calls, conversations, transactions in shops, interviews,
teacher-pupil talk in class, and a host of other events where language is
dominant, are structured. In the field of written texts, discourse analysts
are interested in how bits of text fit together coherently and form patterns,
which, in turn, create whole, completed discourses (for general introduc-
tions, see Coulthard 1985; Cook: *Discourse*, in this Scheme; McCarthy, in
press).

Lexical cohesion

In examining spoken and written discourse, linguists have become increasingly aware of the role of lexis in organizing and creating the regular patterns found in extended stretches of spoken and written language. One type of patterning may be called *lexical cohesion* (see Halliday and Hasan 1976). In written and spoken discourses, vocabulary items re-occur in different forms across boundaries (clause- and sentence-boundaries in writing and, additionally, turn-boundaries in speech). Simple examples would be how, on second occurrences, 'car' becomes its superordinate 'vehicle' and 'gorgeous' becomes its near-synonym 'beautiful' in these examples:

1 Police are examining a *car* parked on the hard-shoulder of the M11 between junctions 7 and 8. The *vehicle* appears to have been abandoned.

2 **Sarah**: *Gorgeous* weather today!
  Mary: *Beautiful*, isn't it!

In either case, the initial words ('car' and 'gorgeous') might have simply been repeated in identical form, but in fact, in discourses, we regularly find *exact repetition* alternating with this feature of *reiteration* or *relexicalization*. It seems especially true in casual conversation that we do not simply repeat one another's words, but recast them, offering our own equivalents, or using superordinates to refer in a more general way to specific items. All this is part of what is often referred to as the *negotiation of meaning*, namely that meanings become fixed in context by the lexical environment created around them by the different speakers, or by a writer varying lexical choice. Here are some examples of how speakers typically negotiate meaning using lexical variation:

1 **Jim**:   I love those Spanish ones.
  Brian: I *like* them . . . wouldn't say I *love* them.
  Jim: Oh I *think they're great*!
  (Brian *downtones* 'love' to 'like'; Jim offers an *equivalent* phrase.)

2 **Madge**: I'm surprised you don't have a *cat*.
  Annie: We never did like *pets*.
  (Annie *broadens* the meaning by using a superordinate.)

3 **Nick**: He's *shy*, really *timid*, you know.
  Lynda: Like a *little mouse*.
  (Lynda fixes the meaning by offering equivalents.)

4 **Bridget**: I like him . . . very *mild-mannered*.
  Liam: Yeah, not at all *pushy*.
  (Liam fixes a precise context by using an opposite.)

The features in our examples are extremely common in conversation, and show how the patterns of lexical cohesion can be related to important functions in speech. We see here how the abstract sense relations described in **2.2** are actually *realized* in the process of creating discourse. Descriptive linguists have only really begun to scrape the surface of the way speakers trade vocabulary items and how and why writers vary their lexical choices, but applied linguists and language teachers must be interested in such observable features as they may have implications for how vocabulary is taught and practised.

▶ ## TASK 44

Pick out repetitions and relexicalizations in this short written text and label them as *exact repetition*, *synonym*, or *superordinate*.

'On the other hand you could become a teacher, a journalist, or perhaps a publisher. These professions often have openings for people with qualifications in language. But the gift of tongues will never make you terribly rich I'm afraid. If you want to get horribly rich you should avoid these mediocrely-paid jobs. Nowadays the jobs that make people wealthy are mostly in the worlds of finance and high-tech. Work in the city and you might end up with a BMW or a Porsche; toil away as a teacher and all you'll get is a clapped-out Fiesta and a mortgage.'

As you did Task 44 you may have wondered whether 'toil away' and 'work' were truly synonymous, or whether they are more, or less, synonymous than 'terribly' or 'horribly' are, or indeed whether the author is implying a deliberate *contrast* between 'toil away' and 'work'. In other words, you were using these features of lexical *cohesion* as clues to creating coherence in the discourse in your mind. Therefore, the kinds of synonymy, antonymy, and superordination we are looking at here are different from the rather fixed and stable relations we described in **2.2**; we are now talking about a discourse-processing *skill*, inferring relations between lexical items in context.

▶ ## TASK 45

Now try and attribute functions to the lexical variations highlighted in these snippets of conversation:

1 **Rick:**   I see Tony's bought a *brand new car*.
  Nora: He loves *status symbols*!

2 **Madge:** That's a *marvellous* gadget.
  Annie: Well, it's *okay* . . . a bit fiddly though.
  Madge: Looks pretty *impressive* to me.

3 **Brian:**   Ray's *a bit of a fool* you know.
  Jim: *A complete idiot* if you ask me.

Topic

So far we have considered lexical cohesion merely in terms of pairs of words linked by some sort of semantic relation and performing some localized function, but often we can trace such relations from one word to another, and to another, until we can see quite complex *chains* in discourses. Such chains enable us to see how *topics* (the subjects people exchange ideas and information about) begin, shift, expand, and close, or perhaps arise and peter out very quickly. It is from many such regular occurrences of topics over many conversations and texts that we are able, intuitively, to talk about the 'vocabulary of a topic', a concept which is often at the forefront of the organization of vocabulary for language teaching purposes, as we shall see in **7.1**. *Topics* are part of our schemata (see **3.4**). As well as knowledge about how people behave at dinner-tables (that they sit rather than stand, that they eat rather than wash, etc.) we know what sort of things they talk about and what areas of interest usually arise (e.g. *holidays*: cost, accommodation, memorable places, etc.). So *topic* is an important psycholinguistic concept. But discourse analysts like to confirm or refute intuitions by examining data, and in the case of topics, repetitions and relexicalization chains can be used to illustrate dominant topics, minor ones, and so on, and to fix the vocabulary that is realizing them. Let us look at some chains in a short conversational extract:

A group of people are talking about the ferry crossing on their recent holiday:

A: but it was lovely our one with the nightclub and we had, we
   had a super cabin which was just below the nightclub ,
   utterly soundproof you know, when you think what houses are
   like, when we shut our cabin door you wouldn't know there
   was anything outside and yet there was a nightclub pounding
   music away, just one immediately overhead and we were
   the cabin next to it and you couldn't hear at all
C: good heavens
B: that's good , very good
A: and it's, of course we could say to the children we'll just be
    upstairs and they knew they just had to put their dressing
   gown on and come up if they wanted us and that was super
C: were you, did you have a car with you?
(*Crystal and Davy 1975:52*)

The words that form chains are 'cabin', 'nightclub', 'soundproof', 'below'/'overhead', and the evaluative 'lovely'/'super'/'good'. The chains break at C's last turn ('did you have a car with you') and a new sub-topic, *car*, comes in to replace the cabin and nightclub. *Children* (see A's last turn) gets taken up again much later in the conversation ('I mean it's probably worth it with *kids*').

► ## TASK 46

Look at this extract from further on in the same conversation about ferries, and draw chains connecting vocabulary which is repeated or relexicalized as (near-) synonyms, antonyms, or superordinates. How would you sum up the topic(s) of conversation in this stretch?

C: I've heard, I mean every summer, you see stories of tremendous queues at the . . .

D: but they're people who haven't booked

A: yeah, and people . . .

D: mind you, last summer there was a weekend when the queues were so bad that even people who'd booked couldn't get on boats

B: and yeah, it was something to do with the strike though wasn't it

D: yeah, there was some trouble as well, yes, that's right

A: but certainly . . .

D: but we've never had any trouble . . .

A: in the past we've just rolled up, if we go Southampton, le Havre or Cherbourg then we book and I do wonder what would happen if for example . . .

D: we haven't been the other way for a few years

A: there are often people who broke down for example, so they missed their booking or their child has been ill so they'd stopped somewhere and they've missed their booking and those people have to wait for a vacancy, in the years we've been they've got on usually, there haven't been masses of people waiting to get on, but the year that we did break down we were actually booked back across from Boulogne or Calais or somewhere and we just drove up and got on to the boat that happened to be there

(*Crystal and Davy 1975:ibid.*)

Lexical signals

Another feature of vocabulary in discourse is the way that some words play a crucial role in organizing the discourse. We can illustrate this by looking at the curiously 'empty' nature of certain words. For example, if I say the following to you in reply to the question 'What did you and *x* talk about?':

'We talked about the problem and some of the issues involved and he suggested an approach that might lead to a solution.'

you would have to already know what the subject-matter of my conversation was, or be a mind-reader, to have any earthly idea whether I was talking about the disposal of nuclear waste, or my marriage, violence in sport, or why the bank refused me a loan. In other words, these items are highly *procedural* rather than schematic (see **4.2**). The vocabulary items in our extract do not seem to be realizing any *topic*, but simply *referring* to a topic and *labelling* the components of the topic in some way. 'The problem' tells you there is a difficulty or negative feature in the situation I am referring to; there are 'issues' (features that raise questions or arguments) and possible ways ('approaches') of getting rid of the problem ('solution'). You, the listener, fill in, or *lexicalize* these 'half-empty' words with reference to other parts of my discourse (things I have said, or say subsequently) or to your knowledge of the situation.

Sentences such as our last example, of course, do not occur dangling in mid-air, but in context, and our particular example is likely to occur in a serious context with reference to a serious problem; it is unlikely that I was talking about a puncture in my bike or why the salt was not coming out of the salt-cellar! We associate sentences such as our example with what we might call *problem-solution* discourses (see Hoey 1983; Jordan 1984). Words like 'problem', 'issues', 'approaches', and 'solution', and their many near synonyms ('difficulty', 'drawback', 'matters', 'questions', 'response', 'answer', 'work out', 'resolve', etc.) are typical *signals* of the problem-solution pattern in discourse, a pattern found in innumerable texts. Signal words tell us the relationship between different segments of the discourse and alert us to the presence of an overall, predictable pattern in the text. Here is an example; an amateur gardener writes to a magazine for advice. The signal words are in italics and their lexicalizations are boxed and linked to them:

Q: I face a particular *problem* with vine weevil in a plant-growing operation. A *solution* I have seen is to mix aldrin into the potting compost. This seems to me an appalling *approach*, given the amount of handling involved. Is there an organic *answer*?

A: Watering with diluted liquid derris works very well

(reader's letter to *Organic Gardening*, August/September 1988)

► TASK 47

Try and add to this list of synonyms for typical signal-words of the problem-solution pattern:

problem, drawback, . . .	(problem)
approach, response, . . .	(response)
result, outcome, . . .	(result)
solution, answer, . . .	(solution)

Problem-solution patterns are very common in academic and technical texts. They are also frequently used by language learners who have to write essays on 'problem' topics (pollution, TV violence, famine, etc.). The signal words are the abstract vocabulary of argument. Sometimes they are fairly easy to translate from one language to another (cf. English, 'problem'/ French, *'problème'*/Swedish, *'problem'*/Spanish, *'problema'*), but other words in English often present difficulty, such as 'issue', 'matter', and 'affair', as do the collocates of some of the signal words, such as 'raise'/ 'present a problem', and 'come up with a solution'.

► TASK 48

Do as in the letter to the gardening magazine: underline the signal words and circle their lexicalizations in this text:

Our motorways are getting more and more congested, and yet no one seems to have any easy answer to the problem. The government's response seems to be to build more and bigger roads but this only seems to bring more and more traffic on to them so that they too rapidly fill up. Should we take a more radical approach and charge tolls or install pay-as-you-drive meters? There are those who believe such measures to be the only long-term solution.

The problem-solution pattern, in its very simplified forms in our examples, is just one of several types of text which have predictable abstract signalling and organizing vocabulary associated with them (see Jordan 1984 for others). Signalling words are not just there to keep topics 'running'; they perform a segmenting function and enable the speaker/ writer to refer *back* to segments of the discourse and to refer *forward*, to 'flag' segments of discourse which will be addressed subsequently. Thus, in the example in Task 48, 'problem' looks back to the first sentence, while 'approach' looks forward and is lexicalized in the words following 'and'.

Expressive vocabulary
When we look at discourse-signalling words in real texts, we can often

observe that they are accompanied by modifiers that express the author's attitudes and evaluations of the content of the text. As well as transmitting content and structuring the message coherently, a writer or speaker has to maintain the receiver's interest and constantly ward off the 'So what?' or 'Why am I being told this?' stance that may be taken up by the receiver. To do this, senders of linguistic messages use words that express the importance or significance of what they are saying, or evaluate it in some way, for example, as 'awful', as 'humorous', as 'scandalous', as 'fascinating', and so on. This extract is a simple example:

'Perhaps the *most important point* to emerge from the London/Liverpool experience is that if they are to attract industry, then urban development corporations need an enterprise zone. London has one; Liverpool has not.' (*New Society*, 28 August 1987:20)

Here 'point' is one of our discourse-signalling words; it is lexicalized in the subsequent text. It is also pre-modified by 'important', which gives more weight in the message to this 'point' than any other that might emerge. 'Important' acts as a focusing word or weighting word. Note also how 'essential' does the same focusing job in the next extract, which is evaluating a proposed government scheme for early retirement:

'A flexible scheme of this kind has a lot to recommend it, because it recognizes the *essential fact* that retirement is a very personal matter.' (*New Society*, 28 August 1987:12)

The writer uses the discourse-signalling word 'fact' as a peg on which to hang the weighting or evaluating words. In this extract, consider the effect if 'sharp' were to be omitted:

'The ESRC's failure to publish the report, or respond to it, has prompted *sharp criticisms*. 'The £50,000 review has ended with a whimper,' one expert protested.' (*New Society*, 28 August 1987:8)

Without the argument and persuasion of the type of journalism found in *New Society* (a British magazine where political and social issues are discussed), the text would certainly lose some of its zest and engagement for the reader. Even in everyday talk, people often pre-modify their discourse-organizing words and talk about '*tricky* problems', '*fascinating* ways' of solving them, and the like. The expressive words set up particularly strong expectations; they provoke the reaction 'why *tricky*, why *fascinating*? Tell me more!'

For the vocabulary teacher or learner, the points in discourse where signalling words and their modifiers occur will become important nodes

for perceiving the speaker's/writer's evaluation of the topic and decisions
concerning textual organization.

Modality

Every discourse, as well as being *about* something, also represents the
sender's stance or attitude to the message in terms of its truth, its certainty
or otherwise, the sender's commitment or detachment from the message,
and so on. This can be illustrated simply by progressively downtoning a
very strongly assertive statement:

That cat definitely ate the cream.	(assertive)
That cat ate the cream.	(neutral)
That cat probably ate the cream.	(downtoned)
That cat possibly ate the cream.	
That cat might possibly have eaten the cream.	↓

These kinds of meanings, reflecting the sender's stance, are *interpersonal*
ones. Interpersonal meanings addressing truth, possibility, and so on are
normally referred to under the heading of *epistemic modality*, as opposed
to meanings addressing such things as obligation and permission, normally
termed *deontic modality* (see Lyons 1977, Chapter 7). Grammarians have
long recognized a closed class of verbs in English which express modality
(the 'modal' verbs: 'must', 'should', 'could', 'may', 'will', etc.), but recent
discourse studies of large corpora of texts have shown that the modal
meanings realized by the modal verbs can also be realized by a large
number of full, lexical words too, in all the major word-classes. For
example, interpersonal meanings of *probability* and *possibility* can be
expressed by those two nouns themselves, as well as other lexical items
such as 'likely', 'likelihood', 'definite(ly)', 'chance', 'potential(ly)', and
'bound to'. Holmes (1983) and Hermerén (1986) both claim that, in their
data, although the modal verbs are frequent, modal items from other
classes (especially lexical verbs and adverbs) are much more frequent than
is normally recognized. In Holmes' data, lexical verbs, adverbs, nouns, and
adjectives (in descending order of frequency) with modal meanings
account for more of the percentage occurrence of modal words in texts
than do modal verbs, in both written and spoken language. Verbs and
adverbs were particularly rich in Holmes' data; they accounted for 53 per
cent of the instances in her spoken data, as opposed to 42 per cent for the
closed-class modal verbs. Typical realizations of these kinds of lexical
modality in English, as paraphrases of the modal verbs, might be as follows
(expressing varying degrees of commitment on the part of the speaker to
the certainty of the event):

Modal verbs: She *might* go on to university.
Lexical modals: There's a | *possibility* | she'll go on to university.
                              | *chance* |
                   Apparently, there's a *chance* she'll go on to
                       university.
                   It *seems* she's *likely* to go on to university.

A wide range of vocabulary expresses certainty, probability, possibility, unlikelihood, and impossibility in English; Holmes' examples include 'bound to', 'obviously', 'quite clear' (that *x*), 'likely', 'seems', 'allegedly', and 'supposedly' (see also Stubbs 1986). The vocabulary of modality is part of the fabric of discourse and represents an important subdivision of the lexicon.

▶   ## TASK 49

Judge the differences in the speakers' attitudes towards the truth or certainty of their statements in these examples:

1 Obviously, he'd been stealing from the company for years.
  Apparently, he'd been stealing from the company for years.
  It seems he may have been stealing from the company for years.
  There's no way he's been stealing from the company!

2 She must be the best novelist of the decade.
  She's absolutely the best novelist of the decade.
  She's arguably the best novelist of the decade.
  It's been suggested she's the best novelist of the decade.

4.4 Register

In the section on discourse, it was mentioned that someone saying 'We talked about the problem and some of the issues involved and he suggested an approach that might lead to a solution' would hardly be likely to be talking about a puncture in a bicycle on their village street-corner, unless they were being deliberately pompous, or witty. So, clearly, vocabulary choice is significantly governed by who is saying what, to whom, when, and why. It is this relationship between the content of a message, its sender and receiver, its situation and purpose, and *how* it is communicated, which is often called *register*. We cannot simply talk about the vocabulary of English as if it were a free-for-all storehouse of half a million items, all equally available to all users on all occasions. The features which restrict our selection of vocabulary are well-captured in Halliday's (1978) model of the components of situations in which language is used, the three key components being *field*, *tenor*, and *mode*:

field: the subject-matter and purpose of a message (e.g. a travel agent's
           brochure selling holidays abroad)
tenor: the relationship between sender and receiver (e.g. boss to employee,
           friend to friend)
mode: the channel of communication (e.g. phone-call, written report, sign,
           or notice)

Fields such as scientific enquiry, academic argument, and some types of
journalism, generate abstract vocabulary of the type in our problem-
solution examples. People talking informally about banal, everyday
problems and difficulties still have a vocabulary to structure their talk
(including 'neutral' words like 'problem' and 'solution') but their
vocabulary will typically include words such as 'snag', 'trouble', 'do about
x', and phrases like 'the thing is', 'what about *x*?' and a host of colloquial
idioms. A recent English advertisement for wood preservative transmits a
technical field in a chatty 'neighbour-over-the-garden-fence' tenor, but still
within the problem-solution textual mode:

'Put ordinary exterior varnish on your doors and window frames and in no
time at all you'll wish you hadn't.
    Wood shrinks and stretches when the temperature and humidity
changes. Ordinary varnish doesn't, so it cracks.
    If you don't strip it off and start again you'll be in real trouble; your
wood will be open to attack from fungus and rot, and quite frankly, it will
look awful.
    So Berger Cuprinol have developed Wood Stain. A new sort of varnish
that breathes and stretches with the wood.
    When it's dry it forms a surface like human skin. It lets moisture out of
the wood, so that when the wood stretches, Wood Stain stretches with it.'
(Advertisement for 'Cuprinol')

Vocabulary choice is probably the major feature which characterizes
registers. Apparent synonyms may often be distinguished on the grounds of
register alone. Obvious examples would be 'kids' and 'children' or 'fags'
and 'cigarettes'; for example, 'fags' would be unlikely to feature in a formal
scientific article on smoking and health.

There is a close relationship between the idea of *field* in a register and the
schematic vocabulary (see **4.2**) of a given subject area (e.g. *gardening*,
nuclear physics, *gymnastics*), in that the schematic vocabulary *realizes* the
field. Similarly, in conversations, 'field' will be recognized through the
topic(s) talked about. A further important point to note is the role played
by *collocation* (see **2.1**) in characterizing particular fields: the collocation
'to cock the shutter' belongs to the field of photography and would be rare
or non-existent outside of this field (on field and collocation see Benson and
Greaves 1981).

► **TASK 50**

Here are two news reports on the same subject. Pick out vocabulary items which characterize the contrasting registers of *popular press* (e.g. newspapers such as the *Daily Express*, the *Daily Mirror*, and the *Sun*) and *quality press* (e.g. the *Daily Telegraph*, the *Guardian*, and the *Observer*):

THIS WAS the moment the host nation scored a knockout over the Olympic spirit.

One of South Korea's favourite sons had just lost a crucial boxing match and they didn't like it one bit.

They stormed into the ring and started a riot—seconds, coaches, security staff, fans, the lot. And Princess Anne saw it all on TV in the Olympic village.

The noble motto of the Olympics preaches the message: *It is not the winning but the taking part. It is not to have conquered but to have fought well . . .*

But that didn't cut much ice with the over-the-top orientals.

Their solution was to get stuck in with the man at the centre of the controversy, New Zealand referee Keith Walker.

The mayhem started after Korean bantamweight Byun Jong-Il lost to Bulgarian Alexandar Hristov on points in front of his home crowd in Seoul.

(*Daily Mirror*, 23 September 1988)

THE New Zealand referee, Keith Walker, attacked in the ring after the defeat of home boxer Jong-Il Byun, has been suspended by the world governing body, together with Byun and five Korean officials. The Association Internationale de Boxe Amateur, controlling body of the sport, took this action within a few hours of what was the worst incident in the history of boxing in the Games. It may not be sufficient to maintain the sport's future within the Olympic movement.

Walker left Korea immediately; threats to his life had been received by the New Zealand Embassy after radio and television reports of the incident.

According to Anwar Chowdry, president of AIBA, there were "some lapses" in Walker's handling of an ill-tempered bantamweight bout in which there were many offences by both boxers.

This incident has come at a particularly awkward time for the sport. The president of the International Olympic Committee, Juan Antonio Samaranch, is opposed to boxing, and in a BBC radio programme this year, suggested that it might be dropped from the Games.

(*Guardian*, 23 September 1988)

The lexical competence of the native speaker includes knowledge not only of single words typically occurring in particular registers but of collocations and multi-word items associated with them too. Most British people will recognize 'delightful residence', 'tastefully modernized', 'compact patio-style garden' and 'having the benefit of full double-glazing' as typical of estate agents' property advertisements; anyone who consistently used such vocabulary in describing their own house in a chatty letter to a friend could only be assumed to be deliberately aping the register of *estate agency* for witty or sarcastic ends. Equally, native speakers of English immediately recognize these examples from Cowie's (1988) data as typical of the journalistic media, in this case the quality British press:

stage industrial action   oppose demands
threaten cuts   sequestrate funds
propose redundancies

What is more, these collocations are even more precisely characterizable as belonging to the field of industrial relations.

▶ TASK 51

Here is a jumble of collocations taken from two different sections of the same newspaper. Separate them into two lists and name the fields they typically belong to:

grand slam   peak performance
transfer fee   put option
pole position   head for relegation
exchange controls   base rate
insider dealing   downward trend
key stakes   defending champion
asset stripping   final lap

You may have found Task 51 very easy, or you may have wondered what registers 'pole position' and 'put option' belong to. Non-native speakers may well be expected to have much greater difficulty in attributing the collocations to particular registers; native speakers can do so only after experiencing many, many texts. In the language learning context, controlling the register dimension of vocabulary will be crucial. In 7.4 we shall look at attempts to do this in English language teaching. Computer analysis is a very good way of getting at the vocabulary of a register. By inputting a selection of texts on a narrowly defined field with similar author–reader or speaker–listener relationships and in chosen modes (e.g. scientific article, informal seminar talk, newspaper report) we can learn much about frequency within a particular register and about how a word's frequency in that register compares with its frequency in a large, general corpus. Conybeare (1986) studied computer jargon by computer analysis and showed how the register 'computerese' has imported words from general English rather than used the typical neo-classical processes of combining Graeco-Latin roots and affixes as so many other branches of science are wont to do. Her examples include compounds such as 'spreadsheet', 'formfeed', 'fanfold' and words of relatively low frequency in general corpora such as 'hack', 'patch', and 'toggle'. In this way, Conybeare's work captures the 'flavour' of a register in its recurring vocabulary.

▶ **TASK 52**

Consider these examples of computer jargon from Conybeare's data. Note which ones are compounds formed with everyday words, which are quite new formations, and which are more typically 'neo-classical' scientific formations:

megabyte	*wealthware*	*hypermicro*
pixel	*checksum*	*keystrip*
vidtex	*downloadable*	*breakpoint*

5 Vocabulary as data for learning

5.1 Frequency

In this section we look at what problems researchers face when they confront large amounts of vocabulary in the form of various kinds of data and try to make systematically meaningful statements about how often and where words occur, and in what sorts of environments. Such studies tell us a lot about why certain words (and certain texts) may be easy or difficult when used in the context of language learning.

▶ ## TASK 53

Somebody offers you a list of what they claim are 'the thousand most frequent words in language x'. What questions would you want to ask them about their list and the way in which it was drawn up? For example, was it computerized?

It seems self-evident that the most frequent words in any language will be the most useful ones for learners of that language, and therefore the best to start off with, in order to give the learner a basic set of tools for communication. But frequency is not as simple a matter as it looks, nor is it likely that any syllabus or coursebook would want slavishly to stick to what frequency lists tell us.

Questions that have to be asked about any frequency list used as a basis for syllabuses or materials include the following:

1 What size corpus was used to get the frequency count?
Billions of words are expended in speech and writing in a language like English each minute of the day, so one may ask whether a corpus of one million words is adequate, or even the twenty million words suggested by Halliday (1966) which the COBUILD dictionary project at the University of Birmingham had at its disposal. Interestingly, lexicographers report that after about five million words, no great new gains are made in information about the more common words, and the patterns of frequency established in the first five million words are repeated and reinforced. What is most likely to happen is that more words with a figure of one or two occurrences will be added to the list.

2 Was the corpus written language, spoken, or both?
Large corpora tend to be based on written language, because this is easy to gather. Speech is ephemeral but vast in the volume of output at any moment in time. The Birmingham corpus uses speech and writing, but the corpus is still predominantly written language. The Lancaster/Oslo/Bergen corpus is taken from printed sources only; it follows, in its choice of texts, the American Brown University corpus (see Hofland and Johansson 1982).

3 Did the corpus cover a wide range of text-types, topics, registers, situations, etc.?
A wide range is clearly advantageous if we want a frequency count for general language teaching. But frequency counts exist for specialist areas too (e.g. science; see Johansson 1978), based on carefully chosen sets of texts, and modest programs now exist which enable individuals to get frequency counts from their own chosen sets of texts on microcomputers.

4 Did the frequency count bunch word-forms together under single entries, or did it separate them? In other words, are 'actual' and 'actually' treated as the same item or as different?
Separating different word-*forms* can often reveal interesting features of frequency; for instance, 'certainly' is much more frequent than 'certain' in the Birmingham corpus (see Sinclair and Renouf 1988). This sort of information often tells us something of the discourse-function of particular word-forms (see **4.3**).

5 How long ago was the corpus assembled; does it contain up-to-date information? For example, in English, we might want information on the frequency of words such as 'computer' and 'video'.
Word-counts become dated. West's *A General Service List of English Words* (1953) contains some meanings in English whose frequency has undoubtedly declined in the last thirty years (e.g. the meaning of 'gay' as 'happy' or 'jolly'). Furthermore, current everyday words like 'refrigerator' and 'television' do not appear.

6 Does the count take into consideration very frequent *multi*-words items? For example, in English, we might wish to know whether 'get up' is more frequent than 'get on', or 'get away with'.
In **1.3**, we saw that multi-word items were very frequent in speech and writing. Many lexical lists that form the basis of coursebooks give us only single words and the more obvious phrases. It is quite difficult to get at the frequency of multi-word items, but one way is to use *concordances*, that is, lists which show a word and its immediate surrounding contexts for every time it occurs in a body of data (see **5.4**). These can also be produced on home-computers, using, for example, the Oxford University Press Concordancing Program, *Micro-OCP* (OUP 1988), relatively easily.

7 Does the count tell us about frequency of *meaning*? If 'book' occurs as a frequent word, how many occurrences were in the meaning of 'reading matter' and how many were in the verb meaning 'to reserve'?

Getting at which *meanings* of a particular word are most frequent is also best done by looking at concordances, where we can see the word in different environments. We can also often see interesting correspondences between the different meanings of an item and the different structural environments in which they occur (see Sinclair 1988). West (1953) gives useful information on different meanings of the same word in the form of percentage frequencies. Here is an example, the entry for 'fat':

FAT	236e		
fat, adj.		(1) A fat man, sheep	
		Fat meat	61%
		(2) *(= thick)*	
		Plant with fat leaves	
		A fat book	14%
		(3) *(figurative)*	
		Fat pastures	
		A fat smile	3%
fat, n.		Cooking fat, beef fat	
		Oils and fats	18%
— — — — — — — — — — — — — — — — — —			
fatness, n., 2e; **fatten,** v., 8e; **fatty,** adj., 10e			

(West 1953: 175)

▶ TASK 54

Opposite is an entry from West, with the percentages for each meaning of the word deleted. Can you make approximate guesses as to which meanings of the word will be most frequent? What factors influence your decisions? Check your guesses against West's percentages, given on page 76.

```
save, v.              1078e    (1)  Save a person from danger
                                    Just saved himself in time
                                    I saved my books from the fire
                                        (= rescued)                    —%
                               (2)  (protect against possible danger or
                                        loss)
                                    A railing to save people from falling
                                    over
                                    God save the King                 —%
                               (3)  (economize)
                                    Save time, trouble, cost
                                    A great saving of time (n.)       —%
                               (4)  (store up against the future)
                                    Save money
                                    Save up (money)
                                    My savings (n.)
                                    The savings-bank (n.)             —%
                               [Save = except,  14% ;  adj.,  saving
                                 grace, etc., 2% ;  prep., saving your
                                 presence, 2% ;  conj., save that, save
                                 to, 2%]
```

(*West 1953: 426*)

5.2 Range

A word (or word-form) may be quite frequent, but a majority, or even all, of its occurrences might be in just one or two texts, in which case, although its *frequency* might look significant, its *range* might be quite small. The useful words for the learner are those words which (a) are frequent and (b) have a fairly wide range, that is, those which occur across a wide variety of texts. Information about range can be presented in the form of statistical comparisons between the occurrence of a word in one part of a corpus (e.g. just the scientific texts in the corpus) and its occurrence in the corpus as a whole. Johansson's (1978) study of the vocabulary of learned and scientific English does just this, giving, in turn, the number of occurrences of a word in the scientific texts of the Brown University Corpus of Present-day American English (see Kucera and Francis 1967) and then a 'differential ratio', which is a figure that compares the occurrences in the scientific texts with occurrences of the same word in the corpus as a whole. Any word that gets a differential of around 16 occurs with more or less the same frequency in the scientific texts as in the whole corpus. Any word with a *lower* differential is not very characteristic of scientific and learned English. Words with *high* differentials are characteristic of scientific and learned English.

Overleaf is a page from Johansson's list. Note that 'have' and 'followed' seem to be, as we would expect, equally common in the scientific/learned and the general corpus (each having a differential of around 16). 'Hypothalamic' with a differential of 100, is highly restricted to the scientific/learned tests. 'Her' (differential of 4) is clearly far less frequent in the learned/scientific texts than in the corpus as a whole.

field	50	18	hard	26	13	intensity	27	48
figure	66	32	hardy	33	79	interest	79	24
figures	38	34	has	431	18	internal	23	37
file	21	26	have	551	14	international	35	23
final	30	19	having	38	14	into	223	12
finally	35	18	he	388	4	involved	33	22
find	50	13	heat	29	30	is	2 409	24
firm	21	19	held	31	12	isolated	22	63
first	243	18	hence	31	53	issue	40	26
five	39	14	her	132	4	it	1 146	13
fixed	27	31	here	85	11	items	31	43
flow	29	43	high	102	21	its	303	14
flux	26	87	higher	45	28	itself	73	24
foam	33	89	highly	26	28	job	27	11
foams	23	100	him	98	4	just	68	8
followed	27	16	himself	32	5	justice	28	25
following	73	33	his	454	6	kind	30	10
follows	40	52	history	26	9	knife	37	49
food	26	18	holder	21	78	know	34	5
foods	23	45	home	28	5	knowledge	27	19
for	1 568	17	house	25	4	known	45	18
force	64	28	how	73	9	labor	37	25
forces	34	19	however	147	27	lack	24	22
form	110	30	human	37	12	land	21	10
formed	28	37	hypothalamic	22	100	language	35	32
former	26	20	I	184	4	languages	25	63
forms	61	48	if	332	15	large	91	25
found	117	22	illusion	25	68	larger	48	39
four	50	14	image	55	46	last	49	7
free	59	23	immediately	30	24	late	24	13
from	792	18	impact	25	37	later	65	16
full	25	11	importance	40	37	latter	43	38
function	81	72	important	82	22	law	91	30
functions	29	60	in	4 097	19	lead	20	16
funds	22	23	inches	43	50	least	62	18
further	59	27	include	30	27	leave	20	10
future	31	14	included	23	24	left	46	10
gain	36	49	including	33	19	length	52	45
gas	42	43	increase	75	38	less	111	25
gave	29	10	increased	52	36	let	51	13
general	114	23	increases	43	60	level	77	36
generally	39	30	increasing	26	35	levels	20	29
get	23	3	indeed	35	22	life	74	10
girls	22	14	independent	28	40	light	62	19
give	58	15	index	72	89	like	88	7
given	103	27	indicate	29	36	likely	54	36
go	34	5	indicated	37	34	limited	33	31
good	47	6	indicates	21	53	line	97	33
government	69	17	individual	75	31	lines	77	39
great	96	14	individuals	25	30	liquid	26	54
greater	54	29	industrial	26	18	list	56	42
group	120	31	industry	60	35	little	63	8
groups	48	38	influence	41	31	living	20	10
growth	53	34	information	126	47	local	72	25
gyro	26	100	initial	24	35	location	20	32
had	331	6	instance	20	24	long	67	9
half	29	11	instead	21	12	longer	34	18
hand	99	14	institutions	20	20	loss	22	26
hands	60	21	intelligence	20	42	low	66	38

(Johansson 1978: 45)

► TASK 55

Pick out three words from the above extract from Johansson with a very high differential. See if any of the dictionaries you or your students commonly use give information about their restricted range.

5.3 Lexical density and variation

► TASK 56

Compare the two extracts below. The first is a transcript of two people talking while they are trying to adjust a door-closure to prevent it from slamming. The second is a written set of instructions accompanying a picture of the door-closure mechanism. What are the main differences in vocabulary between the two?

1 **Mike:**   erm . . . that's too much now, too slow, I'll have to take it back a bit . . . there
   Donna: oh, there's two
   Mike: this one controls the speed
   Donna: I don't mind if it doesn't shut properly at all
   Mike: no, it'll shut, it'll shut . . . so . . . try it now
   Donna: yeah, that's it
   Mike: it's better than it was
   Donna: it'll do

2 The outer screwing mechanism (A) controls the snapshut operation and should be adjusted clockwise to reach the slowest speed while still affecting proper closure. The inner screw (B) adjusts clockwise to control the overall closing speed and may be set to the desired rate of closure. Replace the protective cover and tighten the retaining screws (C and D).

Both extracts in Task 56 are just over fifty words long, but it is noticeable that the written text seems 'heavier' in vocabulary than the spoken one. The spoken text is an example of what Ure (1971) calls 'language-in-action', that is, people are using language as an accompaniment to the action they are engaged in, and the feeling of lightness or heaviness of vocabulary is what Ure calls 'lexical density'. The lexical density of a text can be measured by counting the total words in a text and then counting the *lexical* words, that is, the content words, excluding the grammar or function words, and calculating the lexical words as a percentage of the total words; the higher the percentage, the higher the lexical density. For our two texts, the figures are as follows:

	words	lexical words	lexical density
spoken	51	15	29.4%
written	53	33	62.2%

This is a crude measure, and depends on a number of somewhat arbitrary decisions (e.g. that contractions and hyphenated words will count as one word, and that numerals are 'function' words) but, provided one is consistent, interesting differences can be observed in the vocabulary-loads of different texts. The two speakers adjusting the door had all the physical context in front of them; in such situations the names of actual objects are used less, and a higher number of *deictic* words ('this one', 'there') and pronouns are used. The written text is less dependent on physical context and its words make specific reference to items in the situation. Speaking versus writing is one important dimension affecting lexical density, but some spoken modes (e.g. oral narrative, or a formal lecture) might be lexically quite dense. In Ure's research, the crucial factors creating low lexical density were language-in-action and the fact that there was verbal feedback between one speaker and another (as opposed to lectures, or monologues). Ure's overall findings, though, demonstrated that spoken texts had a lexical density on average of less than forty per cent, and written texts were, on average, over forty per cent.

► ## TASK 57

Do a lexical density count for these short extracts from the same novel. Is the lexical density more or less the same, or significantly different?

1 'The greater part of the morning she had spent alone; but after a while her father joined her. He had fully made up his mind that, come what might, nothing should separate him from his younger daughter. It was a hard task for him to reconcile himself to the idea of seeing her at the head of Mr Slope's table; but he got through it.'

2 'And very becoming her dress was. It was white velvet, without any other garniture than rich white lace worked with pearls across her bosom, and the same round the armlets of her dress. Across her brow she wore a band of red velvet, on the centre of which shone a magnificent Cupid in mosaic, the tints of whose wings were of the most lovely azure, and the colour of his chubby cheeks the clearest pink.'
(Anthony Trollope: *Barchester Towers*)

Lexical density is a statistical measure; it does not tell us how 'difficult' or obscure the words in a text are; the fact that text 2 above may seem to have more 'literary' vocabulary than text 1 is independent of lexical density. Lexical density is determined by text-*type* and is largely independent of text-*length*, though, as with all averaging counts, longer stretches of text are to be preferred in order to produce more reliable averages (see Færch *et al.* 1984:84).

Lexical *variation* takes as its starting point the distinction between *token* and *type*. If a text is 100 words long, it is said to contain 100 *tokens*, but many of these tokens may be repeated within the text and this may give us a considerably lower total of *types*. In the sentence 'She promised him she would write to him and write to him she did' there are 14 tokens, but some are repeated; there are only 8 *types*, ('she', 'promised', 'him', 'would', 'write', 'to', 'and', 'did'). The ratio between tokens and types for this sentence is 14:8; the difference between the two numbers is great, indicating a fairly low load of differing items. In the sentence 'As the trees grow gold and brown, then autumn has come to replace summer', we have 14 tokens *and* 14 types, so the vocabulary load is quite high, with no repetition.

▶ # TASK 58

Do a token-type ratio for this short text:

'They came yesterday to sort out some problem with the phones. The phone in my office has somehow got crossed with the secretary's and they just couldn't work out how the wiring system was, since it was so archaic. They have not solved the problem yet and have to come again tomorrow.'

You may have decided that the text in Task 58 had a fairly high lexical variation, that is, that for approximately every thirteen words, nine were new. But again, certain decisions have to be made in counting which might affect the result: are 'came' and 'come' the same *type*, and is the 'out' of 'sort out', the same 'out' as in 'work out'? Once more, consistency is all important; it is probably sensible for pedagogic ends to treat inflected forms of a word as the same type, and also the two 'outs'. Lexical variation counts do give us a rough measure of how many new items are introduced into a text as it unfolds; this may not be the same as new words (in the sense of words never encountered before) for a language learner, but it can be a useful measure in predicting the likely degree of difficulty a text might present.

At the other end of the scale to gross measures of vocabulary in text, we might wish to concentrate our attention on the contexts in which a particular word occurs in large amounts of data, and it is here that *concordances* come into their own.

5.4 Concordances

Concordances used by language researchers are usually of the KWIC (key-word-in-context) type, where a chosen word-form from a given corpus of data is displayed in all its occurrences with a set number of words or characters either side of the key word, providing a minimal context. Huge computerized corpora such as the Birmingham Collection of English Texts (BCOET) (Birmingham University) and the Survey of English Usage (University College, London) are often consulted using concordancing computer programs, but recently inexpensive software has become available for home-computer use, *Micro-OCP* (OUP 1988). This extract illustrates the appearance of a typical concordance. It is a sample from BCOET of the first forty-five lines for the word 'penny'.

```
ifpenny goes off the manufacturer's profits and a penny goes on to the price probably shared out whe
much had been done to gear up defences since the penny had dropped with the Western govern- ments.
probably fair to look at it that it cost an extra penny halfpenny to ship petrol to Peterborough and
anathema to the Yankee, who wanted to keep every penny he had earned whether honest or dishonest; t
re he thought about it the less he understood it. Penny, he knew, was anything but puritanical. The
trollops resided in this gnomelike skull. It was Penny herself who now appeared upon the scene and
h, ready to exert it to the last man and the last penny if her direct interests are threatened.' Cze
er state of mind because she had suddenly found a penny in the fluff of her raincoat pocket and went
k'? Is it better to live big today or hoard every penny in the bank for tomorrow? Is it better to be
bade her then or ever again to give as much as a penny in con- tribution to the Church. And he a bo
re sure you can build up a pile-you'll need every penny (laugh ) C: Yeah I: Um, it's sort of claustr
postcard when I get there? I shall anyway have a penny left to buy that with.'' Mary jumped to her f
and paid my Union 4d and my rent 3s. ld., I had a penny left! So I threw it across the field. I'd wo
reason On! On! To thirteen thousand pounds.! One penny less is treason. As my guide had predicted,
ry minute coming to tell you of our invita- tion, Penny,'' murmured the clergyman. 'It hadn't arrived
d his wife - '' that bit up by the top there.' The penny now dropped. I recalled great battles with M
but held the male prerogative of receiving every penny of the family's dole money straight into his
) had cheerfully refused to contemplate putting a penny of their own into the development costs. Bef
ing, and Sir Charles's will stipulated that every penny of income should go to charity. The Trustees
no beneficiary under a will may receive a single penny of his inheritance until the funeral parlour
aves of bread). But to Mr Hazel it was worth every penny of it. He became, if only for a few hours, a
ths, the acid, proteinless diet killed him. Every penny of his wages for the entire period was found
Central Europe. Not one British soldier, not one penny+ of British money, must be involved in this
to the customers ((B)) well this it depends which penny of the four and four or four and five of the
he rest myself. You go back to the house now with Penny; oh, and if you change the water in the aqua
er to maintain the egalitarian spirit, and save a penny or two at the same time. And today, because
scm.'' ''Who told you that we were going out today, Penny?'' pro- tested Mr. Dekker mildly, leaning upo
eks!'' ''I didn't know Mrs. Zoyland had a daughter, Penny,'' remarked the Rector gently, looking anywhe
f fourteen <P 46> proposed that there should be a penny reward per hour for e the sun pours over the
tands afore us, among these here 'taties.'' 'Well, Penny,'' said Mr. Dekker with decision, 'I'm afraid
ll the old maids in Silver Street!'' ''But, my dear Penny,'' said Mat Dekker, stretching out his long w
ought, 'I shall get red as a turkey-cock, just as Penny said. My hand will shake when she gives me m
eted her message and came back to the counter. ''A penny stamp, please, Miss Vernon.' The postmistres
not even Philip? '' whispered Mary to John. 'Not a penny,'' the man from Paris answered. ''And what's m
th me, and I would tell him you're not getting a penny, the damn things not being published until
ng made. But nobody closely involved will bet one penny they will succeed. The pipeline's cost is no
trong enough to cook again, he sent me off with a penny to buy him four farthing eggs from a shop up
very single day for the last six months and not a penny to pay?' He turned and walked away towards t
hought they could, as long as the old man 'helped Penny to pump before he came across the road.'' Joh
ddle shovelled them up without a look. The fourth penny tumbled on to number three and my sister smir
ot us at fire-sale prices but also won't pay us a penny until shooting's over?' 'No, I didn't.' I pa
hard, I'd been through the war and I'd married. A penny was what a child had. I wasn't having that.
nd a six.fourteen,another black, and then my last penny wobbled across the board,teetered about for
undred new pennies to this new main unit, the new penny would be worth 1.2 old pennies. The second o
the existing pound, which would mean that the new penny would be worth 2.4 old pennies. Those concer
```

Researchers find such information invaluable. At a glance we can see the following characteristics for 'penny':

1 Of the 45 entries, 10 are the female proper name. This may be interesting cultural information (that Penny is not an uncommon name) but we should want to be sure that our figures are not distorted by, say, the presence of a novel in our corpus with a main character called Penny.

2 Only 14 of the 45 are in the literal meaning of the physical object (the British or Irish copper coin); no fewer than 21 of the 45 use 'penny' in a figurative way to mean 'money' or 'funds' or 'fortune'. Typical of these are 'Sir Charles's will stipulated that every *penny* of income should go to charity' and 'had cheerfully refused to contemplate putting a *penny* of their own into the development costs'.

3 Out of the 45 entries, 7 occur with 'every' before 'penny'; no other individual lexical word occurs as frequently in the immediate environment of 'penny'. The most frequent function word preceding it is 'a'. There are 6 occurrences with some negating expression.

The concordance information for 'penny' could form the basis of a dictionary entry or could inform decisions about what to teach language learners concerning the word's most typical uses. The *Collins COBUILD English Language Dictionary*, based on the very concordances reproduced here, gives us the information noted in 3 above, after basic definitions have been dealt with:

---

2 Penny is also used in negative expressions and with words like 'every' to emphasize that absolutely nothing is spent or that you are referring to absolutely all of a sum of money. ᴇɢ *It won't cost me a penny... Nobody will bet one penny that they will succeed... To Mr Hazel it was worth every penny.*

(Collins COBUILD English Language Dictionary 1987)

▶ TASK 59

Before looking at the concordance overleaf, try and make some predictions about occurrences of the word-form 'striking' (as a verb or adjective). How many different meanings will there be? What will the typical collocates be? Then study the concordance sample from BCOET:

```
then on it is catch as catch can. One of the most striking signs of the increasing power of society
nce the end of the department meeting. It is just striking six, on the brass-faced grandfather clock
man, we see a world totally new.' One of the most striking statements of this theme has come from Ke
orthodox Plaid Cymru to register an; more really striking successes by constitutional means led the
study conclude: "Adoption as an institution is a striking success.' The parents of adopted children
en, up Whitehall, throbs the long boom of Big Ben striking ten: faint, yet fulibodied in a ghostly w
elationships with the physical environment." more striking than this, however, has been the recent
the whole less flamboyant, less brilliant, less striking than the actresses with whom she was surr
ike most snakes, which withdraw their fangs after striking, the boom- slang keeps chewing at the wou
end of life as we know it. A single megaton bomb striking the centre of a large city would create a
angry and tender struggle to keep the twigs from striking the girl's face, emerged triumphantly at
h because they've been over-simplified. The most striking thing to me about this turmoil of public
way still of sightseers' London. And yet the most striking thing about Piccadilly Circus to the nake
gh this stage of insincerity and acting. The most striking thing about Summerhill is this absolute s
tion that exists at that moment. Perhaps the most striking thing about the late paintings is that th
Aren't these magical values bound to be the most striking thing about the work? The difference in v
ns. ((DJ)) William Hague: ((WH)) I think the most striking thing on this issue is the way in which
will come from biology. In fact, one of the most striking things about the tremendous technological
nto view, and all the crooked houses ; and cranes striking up into the sky, like schoolteachers' fin
pushed into acceptance of cruise, as well as the striking victory for the French Left to the south
been eaten, so they have also developed the most striking, vivid colours not just yet llow and blac
used by her own length of experience. What was so striking was her magnificent diction. The musicali
om the patient, Mrs McGowan, a woman with her own striking way with words: "I've heard that cancer i
opt white standards - is revealed in all kinds of striking ways, from Bobby Ken- nedy's assurance th
ou'd be just gorgeous riding. Low-angled dawn sun striking what looks almost like frost covering tho
n the soft yellowish glow, another toubob who was striking with his whip some new black one who was
ly, modern. To our eyes its traditional aspect is striking with its steep-tiled roofs and the decora
? you didn't ask for it;' For safety and support, striking women were banded together in pre-arrange
ations of support for overseas revolutionaries or striking workers, all of which has become an endem
presentation is now not only morally superior to striking your own bargain; I think for the first
```

Even relatively small samples can reveal unexpected patterns in the use of words. These small samples can of course be checked against much larger concordances, or concordances from one corpus could be checked against another. Facts that might never occur to us about a word sometimes leap out at us from concordances. The most striking thing about 'striking' seems to be how often people use the phrase 'the most striking thing about *x*'!

This section of the book has looked at ways of describing, analysing, and explaining vocabulary, as a feature of the language system, as part of our mental linguistic store, and as a feature of language in use. We have seen how linguists have categorized the way words are internally structured; we have considered a lexicon in which multi-word units play an important part, and we have looked at various ways in which vocabulary can be seen as an interrelated *system* of words and phrases. We have also considered various aspects of meaning, extensions of meaning, and how meaning is constructed by language users. But we also saw that it was not enough to consider the description of vocabulary as a system without asking basic questions about words and the mind. We need, as far as we can, to characterize the extraordinary facility of the human mind for processing, storing, and retrieving thousands of vocabulary items. Finally, we considered actual occurrences of vocabulary in writing and speech in different social settings and different discourse-contexts, and the analytical and statistical observations that could be made from the examination of data. In the next section, we shall look at ways in which such insights have been applied in language teaching, and evaluate the methods and products of such applications.

Percentages from the entry in West (1953) reproduced in Task 54: (1) 17 per cent; (2) 24 per cent; (3) 9 per cent; (4) 26 per cent.

Demonstrating vocabulary

6 Selecting what to teach

For many language teachers the broader questions of what vocabulary to teach will be in someone else's hands (syllabus designers, for example), or will have already been determined by the choice of coursebook or other factors. Even so, it should be a matter of great concern to teachers how their syllabuses and materials have been designed, what criteria (if any) have been followed in making decisions about vocabulary content in language courses, and what the goals of particular decisions are. Without addressing such questions, it becomes difficult to evaluate syllabuses and materials, difficult to understand for oneself why particular vocabulary is to be taught, and, often, difficult to explain to learners why they are being asked to learn particular words.

We shall begin by looking at ways in which criteria for selection of vocabulary have been applied in English language teaching, starting with word frequency.

6.1 Frequency and range

Frequency Most frequent words are useful for learners but it depends largely on which data has the frequent words been drawn upon —

In **5.1** we considered the question of word frequency and the advantages and disadvantages of using frequency as a criterion for selection. Most general coursebooks take for granted that the most frequent words in the language must be presented in the early stages of language teaching, and this is a sensible decision, because they offer the learner a survival-level repertoire for comprehension and production. Coursebook writers and syllabus designers have at their disposal a variety of lexical corpora, as well as their own highly developed intuition as to what words form the central core of the language.

Frequency lists need to be approached with caution and careful analysis. The set of questions suggested in **5.1** as being appropriate issues to take into account when studying such lists should be borne constantly in mind in considering the illustrations over the next few pages.

▶ TASK 60

Try and guess what the ten most frequent words are in English. Do this alone or with a partner. Compare your results with other people's guesses. Are the lists the same?

If your list was not the same as other people's, this is not really surprising. Major computational projects such as LOB (the Lancaster/Oslo/Bergen corpus; see Hofland and Johansson 1982) and the Birmingham (BCOET) corpus do not agree either in every detail, though taken as a whole, there is substantial agreement on the high frequency of the most common words.

▶ TASK 61

1 Here are words 65–70 from the 100 most frequent words in the Birmingham corpus. Which of them probably occur with more than one meaning and which meaning(s) of the words would you guess to be most frequent? If possible, check your ideas against the entries for these words in West (1953).

into   some   then   could   now   time

2 Here is a selection of words from the 400–500 frequency band of the Birmingham corpus. Are there any common subjects which emerge? Are there any useful semantic groupings?

problems	*poor*	*hours*	*police*
feet	*ago*	*start*	*friends*
sat	*certainly*	*class*	*late*
parents	*view*	*difficult*	*started*
shall	*stood*	*wife*	*area*
today	*months*	*city*	*death*
ask	*boy*	*bad*	*further*
show	*living*	*minutes*	*table*
business	*countries*	*road*	*held*
coming	*rest*	*longer*	*area*
education	*usually*	*countries*	

Part 2 of Task 61 perhaps illustrates some of the problems with using frequency as a selection criterion. Words from the same subject area are not necessarily of the same frequency and words of similar frequency come from widely different subject areas; so if we want to organize our vocabulary teaching on a subject basis, then the best we can hope for is somehow to work out intuitively, or through studying a limited set of texts (with the help of computer software where this is available), what the most frequent words are in that subject area.

▶ TASK 62

Look at this extract from *Intermediate Vocabulary* (Thomas 1986).
It is from a unit entitled 'Air Travel'. Many of the chapters in the
book are organized topically in this way. This extract is two-thirds
of the unit (the remaining one-third being a grammar exercise). How
well do the vocabulary items chosen for practice reflect your
intuition as to the most frequent words an *intermediate* level student
might need to learn on this topic? Can you think of any omissions
that you would want to be sure your students knew? How might you
go about checking up that this vocabulary really is representative of
actual use?

Air Travel

At the airport Put each of the following words or phrases in its
correct place in the passage below.

> departure lounge   immigration officer   check-in desk
> departure gate   security guard   duty free   board
> departures board   hand luggage   check
> excess baggage   check in   taxi   passengers
> announcement   runway   trolley   security check
> conveyor belt   on board   take off

When travelling by air you have to get to the airport
early in order to (a) _____ about an hour before your
flight. If you have a lot of luggage, you can put it on a
(b) _____ and push it to the (c) _____, where someone
will (d) _____ your ticket and weigh your luggage. If
you have (e) _____, it can be expensive. Your heavy
luggage is put on a (f) _____ and carried away. A light
bag is classed as (g) _____ and you can take it with you
on to the plane. An (h) _____ looks at your passport
and a (i) _____ checks your hand luggage before you
go into the (j) _____ to wait till your flight is called. If
your want to, you can buy some cheap (k) _____
goods here. Then you see on the (l) _____ or you hear
an (m) _____ that you must (n) _____ your plane. You
go through the (o) _____, then there is sometimes a (p)
_____ before you actually enter the plane. When all
the (q) _____ are (r) _____, and when the captain and
his crew are ready in the cockpit, the plane begins to (s)
_____ to the end of the (t) _____. Finally, permission
is received from the control tower and the plane moves
faster and faster in order to (u) _____.

(Thomas 1986: 5)

Richards (1974) is one of a long line of scholars (see Carter and McCarthy 1988, Chapter 1) who have debated fundamental questions about the pedagogical usefulness of frequency lists. The most frequent words are usually the most informationally *empty* words (i.e. grammar/function words) and yet the learner needs to communicate and understand messages with considerable content right from the very beginning. Richards quotes Michea (1953) in support of examining *available* words (*mots disponibles*) as well as just frequent ones. Two words may be more or less equal in frequency but not equally *available*: 'Available words are known in the sense that they come to mind rapidly when the situation calls for them' (Richards 1974). A word may be more available because it represents a concrete object rather than an abstraction, for example.

Sinclair and Renouf (1988) agree with Richards that the most frequent words are not necessarily the most useful for learners and that common sense demands that the most frequent words be supplemented by intuition: 'The additional list will probably include, among other things, words relating to domestic reality, such as days of the week and kinship terms, and other common lexical sets; also further words to refer to physical sensations and personal emotions, and to use in making evaluations' (p. 151).

► **TASK 63**

Look at the first unit of any beginner's course you are familiar with. Can you find any words that do not belong to the 100 most frequent words in the LOB corpus (reproduced opposite)? What seem to be the reasons for including these less frequent words in the very first unit?

the	have	more	Mr AB
of	are	said	made
and	which	out	first
to	her	about	should
a	she	what	over
in	or	up	very
that	you	some	our
is	they	only	like
was	an	my	new
it	were	them	must
for	there	can	such
he	been	into	after
as	one	time	man
with	all	than	much
be	we	could	years
on	their	me	before
I	has	two	most
his	would	then	where
at	when	other	many
by	if	its	well
had	so	these	even
this	no	now	also
not	will	do	being
but	him	may	those
from	who	any	people

Among the words that will be included in the earliest stages in monolingual language courses will be words concerning the management of teaching and learning. Although used everyday in the class these may be quite *infrequent* words in the language as a whole. The very first unit of *The Cambridge English Course* (Swan and Walter 1984) contains a mixture of basic vocabulary and rather infrequent words (e.g. 'pronunciation') which will crop up regularly in class and which will probably catch the eye of the curious student using the book. The teacher may decide to explain these classroom management words right from the beginning (perhaps by translation or illustration) or may choose to ignore them and simply elicit the necessary behaviour from students by, for example, exemplification and gesture. We shall return to the question of classroom vocabulary in **6.3** below.

▶ TASK 64

Make a list of ten common words/phrases used in classroom management. How soon in a beginner's course would you want to teach/explain them?

Range

Teachers frequently have to make decisions (often from intuition) about the likely range of an item in the language as a whole to create a rank-order of importance among different words that crop up in any text. To a great extent, good dictionaries and coursebooks have already done this job. Usage notes in dictionaries informing users that particular words are 'technical' or 'legal' indicate that they occur mostly in a limited section of the corpus, while we trust that well-designed coursebooks for *general* language teaching have also filtered out highly technical or restricted words. But teachers who take their own texts into the classroom in the form of newspaper clippings and so on will often have to decide from experience and intuition which words are likely to have the most useful range. The learner who comes across new words in texts during personal study or reading may wish to know whether an unknown word has a wide or restricted range. Learners in this situation usually have to rely on dictionaries.

▶ ## TASK 65

Look up the following words in two or three different dictionaries, if possible, and see what information, if any, a learner of English could find out about their *range*:

nous   occident   beseech   hereditament

Information on range is given in the published version of the LOB corpus, where one can see at a glance in how many text-types and individual text samples a particular word occurred. For every entry, the first column of figures gives the number of occurrences in the one-million word corpus, the second column tells us how many text-types the word occurred in (the maximum is 15, and the types are listed at the beginning of the published list), and the third column tells us in how many individual text samples a word occurred (maximum 500, the total number of samples in the corpus, each sample being 200 words). 'The', of course, occurs in all 15 types and in all 500 samples. Other words have a more limited distribution. Here are some examples:

	occurrences	text-types	text-samples
students	171	11	45
defence	129	12	49
temperature	104	8	30
data	96	6	30
drill	53	4	7

Table 3

▶ TASK 66

In this sample from the LOB corpus, find some items with limited range, and consider possible reasons why their range is limited.

sections	49	8	36	studies	47	10	35
farmers	49	8	24	crisis	47	10	31
worship	49	8	22	objective	47	10	27
Spain	49	8	20	contains	47	9	35
plane	49	8	17	Germans	47	9	31
earnings	49	7	15	frame	47	9	29
approximately	49	6	34	universal	47	9	28
limits	49	6	26	centres	47	9	27
electrical	49	6	20	we're	47	8	39
ourselves	48	15	41	recommended	47	8	37
youth	48	14	38	laughed	47	8	34
inner	48	13	39	o'clock	47	8	32
suspect	48	13	37	flow	47	8	28
accident	48	13	35	folk	47	8	25
steady	48	12	38	league	47	8	21
suggestion	48	12	38	dependent	47	7	30
pale	48	12	34	poetry	47	7	18
vision	48	12	32	camp	47	7	17
14	48	11	43	Mrs AB	47	7	14
accompanied	48	11	40	examinations	47	7	10
huge	48	11	39	Congo	47	6	16
address	48	11	36	drugs	47	6	12
rooms	48	11	36	Philip	47	6	12
guests	48	11	35	curve	47	4	14
darkness	48	11	32	0	47	2	13
liberal	48	11	28	comfort	46	14	39
breakfast	48	11	27	sad	46	14	37
tall	48	10	43	admit	46	13	44
enable	48	10	42	named	46	13	43
they're	48	10	37	spot	46	13	42
fourth	48	10	33	affect	46	13	41
calculated	48	10	32	firmly	46	13	41
yours	48	10	31	properly	46	13	39
establish	48	9	43	exciting	46	13	37
maintained	48	9	37	undoubtedly	46	13	37
Italy	48	9	33	visited	46	13	36
prayer	48	8	20	conduct	46	13	35
rent	48	8	19	sharply	46	13	34
Belgian	48	7	15	path	46	13	32
retirement	48	6	12	gentleman	46	13	29
Christ	48	5	15	personally	46	12	38
households	48	3	7	keen	46	12	36
curious	47	14	42	safety	46	12	29
happens	47	14	42	presumably	46	11	39
conscious	47	14	34	surprising	46	11	39
satisfied	47	13	40	cash	46	11	33
protest	47	13	33	improvement	46	11	33
noise	47	13	31	Roman	46	11	33
enthusiasm	47	12	39	accounts	46	11	32
tells	47	12	38	protection	46	11	32
grow	47	12	37	feels	46	11	31
honour	47	12	37	skin	46	11	27
brilliant	47	12	36	craft	46	11	26
sheet	47	12	36	stamp	46	11	15
message	47	12	31	13	46	10	38
glance	47	11	41	attended	46	10	37
seek	47	11	41	recorded	46	10	37
thousands	47	11	40	arrangement	46	10	31
credit	47	11	38	gallery	46	10	29
finish	47	11	35	doctors	46	10	26
examined	47	11	34	premises	46	10	22
oil	47	11	32	emphasis	46	9	32
sell	47	11	32	custom	46	9	28
representative	47	10	36	weapons	46	9	25
16	47	10	35	recovery	46	9	20

6.2 Learnability

Ease or difficulty in the learnability of vocabulary is not unconnected with the notion of frequency, since the most frequent words will probably be absorbed and learnt simply because they occur regularly. But words may be easy or difficult for a variety of other reasons, and may need special attention or focus in teaching.

1. Words may present spelling difficulties. Even native speakers of English have difficulty remembering whether single or double consonants appear in words like 'occurrence', 'parallel', and 'beginning'. Languages with more regular spelling patterns (e.g. Spanish) present fewer difficulties of this kind.

2. Words may present phonological difficulties, either because they contain awkward (for the learner) clusters of sounds (e.g. English 'thrive', 'crisps'), or because spelling interferes with perception of what the sound is (English 'worry' is regularly pronounced by learners as if it rhymed with 'sorry'). Such words may be effectively learned in all other respects, but pronunciation may remain a long-term difficulty, especially where old habits are ingrained.

3. The syntactic properties of words often make them difficult. In English, 'want' presents fewer syntactic difficulties than 'wish': 'want' is followed by an infinitive and/or an object; 'wish' may be followed by a variety of verb patterns in 'that' clauses, as well as by the infinitive.

4. Words may be perceived as very close in meaning by the learner, and therefore difficult to separate one from another. 'Make' and 'do' are notorious in this respect in English. Learners of Spanish often find it difficult to separate '*ser*' and '*estar*', which to the English-speaker seem both to mean 'be'.

5. For specific target groups, words may be 'false friends'. '*Aktuellt*' in Swedish and '*actuellement*' in French do not mean the same as English 'actually'; this false similarity may place difficulties in the way of learning a word.

6. Learners may be unable to relate the meaning of a word to their world experience or to their culture. It may be difficult for learners of English to relate 'solicitor', 'chaplain', or 'estate agent' to anything in their own cultural environments. Such words may for long remain only vaguely or half-comprehended.

The difficulty, or lack of difficulty, a word presents may override its frequency and/or range, and decisions to bring forward or postpone the teaching of an item may be based on learnability. Presentation will also be affected by difficulty and learnability. Published materials handle features of learnability and difficulty in different ways.

▶ TASK 67

Why might the following English words be difficult for a learner? Refer to points 1–6 on page 86, and add any further criteria of difficulty you think are important:

curate   throw   marvellous   tell   evidently   let
questionable   borrow   responsibility

Pender (1988) researched her students' impressions of ease and difficulty in dealing with new words and found, naturally, a certain amount of individual variation alongside general trends. This student's responses to part of a questionnaire are typical of the batch:

Q: What kinds of words are easiest for you in English? Give examples.
A: The words which are similar in Spanish—
   refrigerator—*refrigerador*
   comfortable—*confortable*
Q: What kinds of words are most difficult for you in English? Give examples.
A: The words which are like two words—
   breakthrough—childhood

▶ TASK 68

Either:
write down five words in any foreign language you know, and then consider whether the words were easy or difficult for you to learn, and for what reasons.
Or:
pick five words at random from any learner's dictionary, and consider how easy/difficult they might be for a learner, and why.

Difficulty and learnability cut right across the notions of frequency and range. We cannot predict that just because a word is frequent it will be learnt quickly and thoroughly or, conversely, that, because a word is infrequent, it will not be easily learnt.

6.3 Learners' needs

Predicting what learners will need in the way of vocabulary is important in selecting what to teach; equally important is 'creating a sense of need for a word' (Allen 1983:90), and recognizing that learner perceptions of need may conflict with the teacher's perceptions.

So there seem to be three principal ways in which the selection of vocabulary can be influenced:

1 Teachers'/coursebook writers' predictions.
2 A sense of need in the learner, fostered by the teacher.
3 The learners' own sense of their needs, which may conflict with the teachers' perceptions.

In relation to 1, Allen offers four questions that need to be answered in order to predict learners' vocabulary needs:

1 Which words must students know in order to talk about people, things, and events in the place where they study and live? (When such words are learnt, the new language can immediately be put to use.)

2 Which words must the student know in order to respond to routine directions and commands? (The vocabulary for 'open your books' and 'write these sentences' and other routine instructions should be learnt early, so that such frequently repeated directions can always be given in English.)

3 Which words are required for certain classroom experiences (describing, comparing, and classifying various animals, for example, or having imaginary conversations with speakers of English, or writing letters to pen pals)?

4 Which words are needed in connection with the students' particular academic interests? (Those who will specialize in science need vocabulary that is different from those who plan business careers.)
(*Allen 1983: 108*)

▶ # TASK 69

Make a list of ten words which a young learner of English (aged 16–20) on a short summer course in England, living with an English family, might need in relation to Allen's question 1.

Gairns and Redman (1986) offer ways of tackling the commonest classroom management items, which Allen's second question refers to, and extend the vocabulary of frequent directions and commands to include words like 'tick', 'blank', and 'underline', which often occur in coursebook exercises. Here is an example of a presentation:

time	6.30
place	Rome
reason	tourism

√ There is a tick at the beginning of this sentence.
In this sentence the word <u>dog</u> is underlined.
There are two blanks in the next sentence.
My .... lives .... Venezuela.
In the next sentence the blanks are filled in.
My brother lives in Venezuela.
The fifth word in ~~this~~ sentence is crossed out.
2 + 2 = 4 is true. 2 + 2 = 5 is false.
At the side of this piece of paper there is a map of Italy.
At the top of this piece of paper there is a chart.
I am going to leave out one word in the next sentence.
I come to .... by bus.
I left out the word 'school' in the sentence above.

ITALY

© 1986 Cambridge University Press

(*Gairns and Redman 1986: 62*)

Most currently popular beginners' coursebooks recognize the need to equip the learner with the basic core of the language (the most common grammatical and lexical words) and a *survival* vocabulary which covers Allen's questions 1 to 3. If we survey two currently available courses (Swan and Walter 1984, and Willis and Willis 1988), we find in the first unit of the very first book many basic lexical items which occur in both of them, including 'hello', 'goodbye', 'name', 'where', 'what', 'am', 'is', 'I', 'you', 'from', and the names of countries and nationalities, along with classroom words giving instructions for exercises and activities.

Developing a 'sense of need' for a word may not always be easy, but most students will probably be motivated enough to acquire at least the words given in the list above, and will see the obvious usefulness of the two or three hundred most common items in the language.

Gairns and Redman emphasize the importance of seeing the working out of needs as a collaborative process between teachers and learners. Students often have a keen sense of particularly difficult and/or interesting *formal* areas of vocabulary, and when learning a language like English, will often feel a need to tackle areas such as 'idioms' or 'phrasal verbs'. It would be a pity to ignore such motivation where it exists just because one is committed to a topic-based approach. Consequently, some materials offer a healthy balance of topical and formal headings for their vocabulary components, enabling teachers to respond to these different types of need that learners may feel. Fowler (1987) does this by devoting half of his book to topics and half to specific lexical items which commonly present formal and semantic difficulties. Soars and Soars (1986 and 1987), at both intermediate and upper-intermediate levels, offer headings under 'Vocabulary' which include:

Television programmes   Phrasal verbs
Holidays   Parts of the body
Antonyms with prefixes and suffixes   Homonyms and homophones
Dictionary work

What at first sight appears a jumbled, even confused, list probably captures the varied types of student need admirably.

▶ TASK 70

Look at any general coursebook or vocabulary materials you use or know.

1 How is the vocabulary presented?
   – under topic-headings (*television, holidays*)?
   – under semantic headings (*synonyms, homophones*)?
   – under formal headings (*phrasal verbs, compounds*)?

2 Does the material offer the opportunity to respond to varying perceptions of needs on the part of learners?

3 What deficiencies does the material have in this respect?

Learners have individual senses of need which perhaps do not coincide with those of the group or class. The challenge here is to enable the individual to pursue his or her interests in the way which is most *productive*. Exercises and activities can combine the collective and the individual. Gairns and Redman (1986:57) suggest, alongside conventional vocabulary work on a text, allowing students to choose any words they wish from a text and, within a given time limit, to work on them using a dictionary. In this way learners are encouraged to recognize their own needs, and are assisted in developing their ability to pursue those needs in organized and productive ways.

7 Organizing vocabulary

Once broad decisions have been made concerning the selection of vocabulary, frameworks for its presentation have to be considered. These vary greatly in published materials, but almost all materials explicitly or implicitly reflect notions about the organization and functioning of vocabulary.

7.1 Topic

The use of topic as a framework for vocabulary presentation is very common in materials. We have seen how Thomas's (1986) *Intermediate Vocabulary* used 'Air Travel' as a topic heading to present a selection of connected words (see **6.1**). However, topic may be a problematic framework for several reasons:

1 It is difficult to actually define a 'topic'. What does 'air travel' include? 'Topic' in this sense might derive from particular schemata (see **3.4**): being at airports and doing predictable things ('checking in', 'boarding'), and names of people and things associated with those actions ('stewardess', 'baggage'); but does the topic include 'accidents', 'reading matter', 'crowded toilets', 'boredom'—where does one stop? What people typically talk about when they talk about air travel may be different from words associated with parts of aeroplanes, or customs and immigration rules.

2 Which topics are going to be most useful for learners anyway? 'Moving house' may not be of great interest to younger learners, and 'pollution', although an area of public concern, may be less useful than 'entertainments' for the average learner. The problem is that we cannot hope to cover more than a fairly arbitrary selection of topic headings in a language course.

3 It is difficult to predict exactly what words are the most frequent or useful within any given topic (see **6.1**). To a certain extent this can be overcome by computational analysis of a range of texts on a common topic.

4 On the other hand, topics relate more readily to people's experience than, perhaps, semantic or formal categories may do, for example, the semantic fields discussed in **2.3**, and, carefully chosen, can give a structure to vocabulary teaching which learners are able to perceive and understand.

► TASK 71
Make a list of ten topic-headings for a ten-week, one-hour-a-week vocabulary development course which you feel would be most useful for a group of lower-intermediate learners of English. Compare your results with a colleague's and discuss the differences. What factors determined your choice?

Topic-based materials rarely present *only* words which are topic-specific. Redman and Ellis's (1989) *A Way with Words*, in a unit headed 'Time and Money' also present words such as 'scheme', 'adopt', 'demonstrate', and 'proposal', alongside words like 'borrow', 'afford', and 'occasionally', which have more obvious connections with 'time' and 'money'. Closer focusing on topic is aimed at in Sim and Laufer-Dvorkin's (1984) *Vocabulary Development* by using (in some units) the technique of presenting two texts, one easier, one more difficult, on the same topic and by concentrating attention on words of relevance to academic English, words with maximum 'generative quality', and inherently difficult words. But here too, the practised words are not necessarily topic-specific, and relate more often to the aim of developing general academic vocabulary. For example, in a unit on 'Intelligence', the following exercise is given; in it only the words 'bright' and perhaps 'eccentric' seem obviously related to the overall topic:

Exercise 2
The following words are taken from the two texts. Next to each one write a word of opposite meaning. Use a dictionary if necessary. The first pair is done as an example.

1 hypothetical	*real*	5 numerous	_____	
2 particularly	_____	6 bright	_____	
3 eccentric	_____	7 discrepancy	_____	
4 layman	_____	8 resemble	_____	

(*Sim and Laufer-Dvorkin 1984:68–9*)

This is probably inevitable, since no topic can be considered entirely schematically without consideration of the procedural vocabulary that gives it internal structure and coherence (see **4.2**).

7.2 Meaning

In **2** we surveyed two ways of looking at the meaning of words: one was lexical relations (**2.1 to 2.3**) and the other was componential analysis, or CA (**2.6**). Both have in common the idea that word-meaning can be described internally, within the system of language itself, rather than by pointing to entities in the real world. Lexical relations such as synonymy, hyponymy, and collocation describe words in terms of one another within systematic sets of related words. Componential analysis describes words in terms of shared and non-shared semantic features, these features themselves being only expressible as words (e.g. '+ human', '+ hairy', etc.).

The idea that such systematic descriptions might be useful in the teaching of languages has gained currency over the last decade or so, and has found its way into materials.

► ## TASK 72

Færch *et al.* (1984:88) identify three structuring principles for learners' vocabulary:

1 The learner relates L2 words to the world.
2 The learner relates L2 words to L1 words.
3 The learner relates L2 words to other L2 words already known.

To which of these principles do you think CA and lexical relations are most relevant and why?

Channell (1981) takes the grid-type of representation of meaning used in CA and considers it as a means of transmitting information on meaning in vocabulary teaching. Grids usually consist of a list of features or properties on the horizontal axis and a set of words related by some common component of meaning on the vertical axis. The plus-signs as used in CA can then be filled in to give an at-a-glance view of the shared and non-shared features of the words in the set, as in Channell's grid for 'being surprised':

	affect with wonder	because unexpected	because difficult to believe	so as to cause confusion	so as to leave one helpless to act or think
surprise	+	+			
astonish	+		+		
amaze	+			+	
astound	+				+
flabbergast	+				+

(*Channell 1981*)

The grid can be either a presentational device from the teacher or coursebook, or a way for a learner to organize a vocabulary notebook, or used as a testing device.

► ## TASK 73

Draw up a list of what you think might be the advantages and disadvantages of a grid such as the one for 'being surprised'.

Some criticisms that might be levelled at grids of this sort are that the language describing the features on the horizontal axis is cumbersome, and that while grids may be useful for visual reference, they are difficult to commit to memory and are not of much use when one is searching for a word in real-life communication. On the other hand, they do have an economy that separate dictionary searches for the words listed on the vertical axis cannot offer. What is more, they can be added to as more words are encountered: when 'staggered' comes up it will find its place on the grid, with a profile close to 'flabbergast' and different from 'amaze', for example. The basic grid method is exploited to the full in *The Words You Need* books (Rudzka *et al.* 1981, 1985), where not only CA but collocation is presented by this technique; here is a collocational grid for three words:

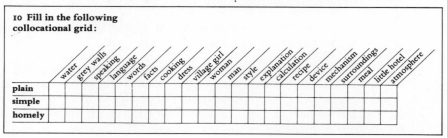

10 Fill in the following collocational grid:

(*Rudzka* et al. *1981:133*)

and the CA grid for the same three words:

6 Being simple

	not rich, ornamental or patterned	straightforward	unattractive (of people)	with nothing added	uncomplicated	without sophistication or education	not having much brains	not difficult	comfortably informal	warm and friendly
plain	+	+	+	+						
simple	+				+	+	+	+		
homely									+	+

(*Rudzka* et al. *1981:129*)

► ## TASK 74

Fill in the CA grid with plus signs where appropriate to illustrate the meanings of this group of 'vehicle names':

	carries passengers mainly	carries cargoes mainly	usually has side windows	seats many passengers	can carry huge loads
car					
van					
bus					
lorry					

Elaborations of the grid method are suggested by Pearson and Johnson (1978) and Harvey (1983). Pearson and Johnson are concerned with vocabulary in reading comprehension and how the concepts which words represent are related to one another. They suggest that concepts are not randomly related but follow predictable lines. Word-association phenomena (see **3.2**) bear this out. A word such as 'dog' is readily associated with other words such as 'cat', 'bark', 'Fido' (or any dog's name), 'collie', 'bite', and 'animal' (1978:25). These associations represent relations such as class membership (dog—animal), 'example of' (Fido), and 'property of *x*' relations (dog—bark/bite). These relations (not unalike, in their complexity, the encyclopaedic networks proposed in **3.2**) can be represented in a *semantic map*, with simple 'is a', 'does', 'has', and 'example of' relations, between nodes. The semantic map for 'dog' looks like this:

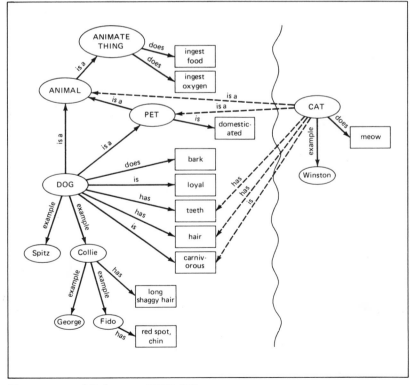

(*Pearson and Johnson 1978:28*)

The 'dog' map might seem far too complex to use in a classroom, and Pearson and Johnson intend it principally as an illustration of the comprehension process, but simplified versions of the semantic map can be devised, using the basic idea of nodes and connections between them. Redman and Ellis (1989:6) use the map technique for an exercise on the '*has* or *is associated with* types of relation' for houses and their contents:

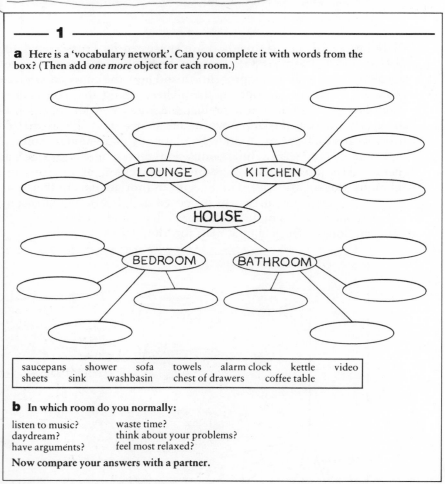

——— 1 ———

a Here is a 'vocabulary network'. Can you complete it with words from the box? (Then add *one more* object for each room.)

| saucepans | shower | sofa | towels | alarm clock | kettle | video |
| sheets | sink | washbasin | chest of drawers | coffee table | | |

b In which room do you normally:

listen to music?   waste time?
daydream?   think about your problems?
have arguments?   feel most relaxed?

Now compare your answers with a partner.

(*Redman and Ellis 1989:6*)

▶ TASK 75

Try to set up grids like Channell's 'being surprised' grid (page 93) for these two groups of words:.

disappointed	*fry*
disillusioned	*boil*
frustrated	*roast*
dissatisfied	*bake*
dejected	*grill*

Work in a group if possible and note the difficulties you encounter. How could you use these grids in class?

Maps and grids are one way of presenting words according to meaning-relations. They can be used as visual presentation devices, as gap-filling activities, for group-work (in discussing alternatives or comparing results), as reference devices, or as a recording device in the vocabulary notebook. They offer no guarantee that the words will be better remembered or more correctly used, but they do offer an alternative to the disorganized word-list or the more conventional ways of arranging related words in lists of synonyms, antonyms, and so on. Many materials are organized partly on semantic lines. A typical example is Seal (1987:16), where the lexical field of 'seeing and sight' is realized in mini-contexts:

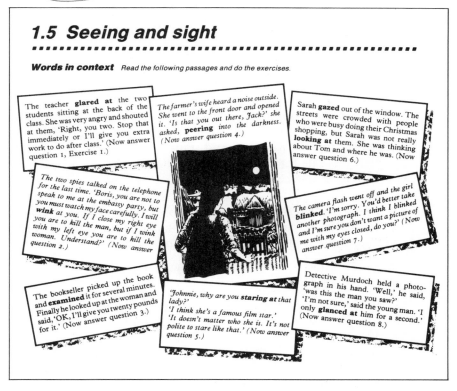

1.5 Seeing and sight

Words in context   *Read the following passages and do the exercises.*

The teacher **glared at** the two students sitting at the back of the class. She was very angry and shouted at them, 'Right, you two. Stop that immediately or I'll give you extra work to do after class.' (Now answer question 1, Exercise 1.)

The farmer's wife heard a noise outside. She went to the front door and opened it. 'Is that you out there, Jack?' she asked, **peering** *into the darkness. (Now answer question 4.)*

Sarah **gazed** out of the window. The streets were crowded with people who were busy doing their Christmas shopping, but Sarah was not really **looking at** them. She was thinking about Tom and where he was. (Now answer question 6.)

The two spies talked on the telephone for the last time. 'Boris, you are not to speak to me at the embassy party, but you must watch my face carefully. I will **wink** *at you. If I close my right eye you are to kill the man, but if I wink with my left eye you are to kill the woman. Understand?' (Now answer question 2.)*

The camera flash went off and the girl **blinked**. *'I'm sorry. You'd better take another photograph. I think I blinked and I'm sure you don't want a picture of me with my eyes closed, do you?' (Now answer question 7.)*

The bookseller picked up the book and **examined** it for several minutes. Finally he looked up at the woman and said, 'OK, I'll give you twenty pounds for it.' (Now answer question 3.)

'Johnnie, why are you **staring at** *that lady?'*
'I think she's a famous film star.'
'It doesn't matter who she is. It's not polite to stare like that.' (Now answer question 5.)

Detective Murdoch held a photograph in his hand. 'Well,' he said, 'was this the man you saw?' 'I'm not sure,' said the young man. 'I only **glanced at** him for a second.' (Now answer question 8.)

(*Seal 1987:16*)

Exercises activating relations such as meronymy and hyponymy (see **2.2**) are found in the same book, in typical classifying exercises:

Exercise 3

Match the parts of animals on the left with the definitions on the right.

1 _____ wing   a) a bird's mouth

2 _____ fur   b) a part which sticks out at the end of an animal's body

3 _____ tail   c) thick hair on the bodies of some mammals

4 _____ feather   d) one of the sharp, hard points on the feet of some birds and mammals

5 _____ beak   e) part of an animal which is used for flying

6 _____ claw   g) one of many parts of the covering that grows on a bird's body

Dictionary work

Put each animal in one of the four columns. Do as many as you can and then check your answers in a dictionary.

| shark | crocodile | parrot | owl | wasp | mouse |
| goat | seagull | fly | lizard | beetle | tiger |

insects	birds	fish and reptiles	mammals

(*Seal 1987:61*)

Collocation can be approached in a variety of ways. At the advanced level, McCarthy *et al.* (1985:158) offer straightforward gap-filling; at the intermediate level, Redman and Ellis (1989) also have collocation activities, this one for distinguishing between different words connected with travel:

---

1. Choose words from the list to complete the sentences which follow it. You will need certain words more than once, and some words you will not need at all. Use your dictionary to help you.

travel   cruise   trip   voyage
journey   tour   expedition

a. We went on a sightseeing .... round London.
b. We're going on a day .... to the country.
c. The return .... from Spain took 36 hours.
d. We went on a Mediterranean .... and the ship was very comfortable.
e. At the moment he's away on a business ....
f. We had a good flight but the train .... was awful.

(*Redman and Ellis 1989:41*)

► TASK 76

It is a fact of English that we say 'tall man/woman', 'tall building', 'tall tree' and 'high speed', but not *'high man/woman', *'tall temperature' or *'tall position'. Do you think a grid would be a useful way of teaching the collocability of 'high' and 'tall'? If so, make one up, or else devise some other kind of activity or exercise.

V Whether using grids, maps, or classified lists, all the materials we have considered here organize vocabulary for teaching in terms of lexico-semantic relations, as opposed to topics (see **7.1**). These are important, but they are not the only ways of organizing vocabulary for teaching. Lexical *form* can also be exploited.

► TASK 77

Look at materials you use to see if any of the vocabulary content is organized in terms of lexico-semantic relations. If it is not, can you see ways in which it could be adapted to include this dimension?

The various exercises and presentation devices illustrated from published materials attempt to visualize the semantic relations described in **2.2** in some way. We see, for instance, that tree-diagrams (see page 19) are not the only way to represent the hyponymy relationship. Descriptive linguists tend to use diagrams of the type found in academic texts; language teachers must be open to alternative modes of presentation and be ready to evaluate the efficacy of different types.

7.3 Form

In **1.2**, it was argued that exploiting the internal structure of words is a useful organizing principle for vocabulary teaching. The study of word-formation reveals that a relatively small number of processes are regularly used to create a large number of new words in a language like English, and that educated native speakers can perceive within derived words the presence of roots, prefixes, and suffixes and can attach meanings to derivations which they have never encountered before. Similarly, native speakers know the conventional meaning of opaque compounds (see **1.3**) and other multi-word units, and can make intelligent guesses at the meanings of new or unknown lexical units.

While language learners might never achieve the same degree of competence as a native speaker with regard to the creation and understanding of derived and compound forms, a good deal can undoubtedly be gained by an awareness of the word-formation processes of the target language. Also, as was claimed in **3.2**, research suggests that native-speaker storage and retrieval of vocabulary is based on double-entry principles, one element of the mental lexicon being whole derived and whole compound words stored as ready-made units, and another element being the set of affixes and basic roots that combine to form new words.

▶ **TASK 78**

Consider any second or foreign language that you know from the point of view of how it forms new vocabulary. Are its word-formation processes similar to English? Are some processes more frequent or less frequent than in English? What problems do you envisage that a speaker of that language would have in trying to learn English?

There is a finite number of affixes in English and some are much more common than others. The commonest ones and their typical meanings can be introduced and taught directly at a relatively early stage. Ellis and Ellis (1983:55) offer an exercise at pre-intermediate level matching suffixes with word-classes, while Swan and Walter (1985:103) use a matching exercise and a word-building exercise at lower-intermediate level to introduce the /ə/ suffix (written as '-er' and '-or') indicating the agent of an action or process. Such decisions are sensibly based on what is likely to be most useful to learners and what they can most easily generalize from; the /ə/ suffix can, for example, be attached to almost any verb in English and is highly productive.

▶ **TASK 79**

1 List the following affixes in order of priority for teaching purposes.

2 Which could be introduced at elementary, pre-intermediate, or intermediate level, and which are best left to more advanced levels?

3 Which are most/least productive?

-ose as in *verbose, jocose*
-ly to make adverbs, as in *quickly, nicely*
re- as in *re-do, re-write*
un- as in *unclear, untidy*
ill- as in *ill-tempered, ill-conceived*
-ing to make nouns, as in *smoking (is prohibited), reading (helps you learn)*
de- as in *demist, derail*

Compounding can also be introduced very early on. Swan and Walter (1984:125) introduce a selection of noun compounds in the beginner level book of their *Cambridge English Course*. As learners progress, they can be encouraged to be more creative. Soars and Soars (1986:63) offer a three-part exercise for intermediate level whose third part is quite open-ended.

---

1 Can you guess the words? Check in the dictionary to see if you're right.

a. What do you use to clean or wash the following?
   your teeth/shoes/clothes/dishes
b. What do you have in your hands for these sports?
   tennis/golf/fishing/squash/
   hockey/baseball
c. Make as many compounds as you can with these words the *second* word.
   cup/glasses/book/bottle/card/
   paper/machine

(*Soars and Soars 1986:63*)

The essence of more open-ended exercises is that it does not matter if the learners produce non-existent new forms; they can be taught to identify these by being asked to consider typical compounds in their L1 (though this may be less than straightforward for speakers of languages where direct compounding is not common); they can also check their creations against a good dictionary or consult the teacher as informant. Decisions about what types of compounding to practise will once again be based on generalizability and utility: in English, for example, the noun + noun compound is common and highly productive.

► **TASK 80**

Rank these compound types in order of productivity and usefulness for teaching:

adjective + noun, as in *blackmail, small-talk*
verb + noun, as in *pickpocket, Walkman*
verb + verb, as in *freeze-dry, make do*
verb + particle, as in *look up, drop by*
particle + noun, as in *off-day, by-product*

How well do you think the exercises on compounds illustrated above adapt themselves to these compound types? Consider some other possible exercises for them.

When we look at language coursebooks, the general consensus seems to be that the learning of derived and compound words *as whole units* precedes analysis of the words into their morphemic structure or consideration of the processes that have formed them. Thus the very first beginner's lessons of Swan and Walter (1984) have formations such as 'surname', 'shop assistant', 'housewife', 'artist', and 'electrician' with no comment on their internal structure. The *COBUILD English Course, Book 1* (Willis and

Willis 1988) goes even further, and considers word-forms in their own right as lexical items, with detailed attention to the various forms a word might take or combine with, and the meanings of these forms, rather than to word-formation processes.

7.4   Contextual relations: register and discourse

The study of registers and the analysis of discourse are both ways of relating language to the context in which it is used, and it is sometimes difficult to separate the two. In general, register studies are concerned with aspects of a situation which feed into language choice, while discourse analysis looks at the processes whereby language acquires meaning in contexts, the forms and products of those processes, the types of texts that are produced, the structuring of exchanges in spoken interaction, and so on (see Widdowson 1983:28, and also Cook: *Discourse*, in this Scheme). In **4.3** and **4.4**, we attempted to make a practical separation of the two, and to illustrate how lexical choice functioned in the creation of registers and the organizing and structuring of discourses.

In discussing register, we were concerned with the role of vocabulary in evoking certain *fields* (e.g. *sport, financial news*), in characterizing relationships between participants, that is, the *tenor* (e.g. *formal/informal, power/equality*), and in characterizing the *mode* (e.g. *spoken/written, lecture/love-letter*).

Most teachers are probably fully cognizant of the dangers of violating register constraints by the misuse of vocabulary, and make sure that learners are aware of the appropriate contexts for words: for example, that 'precipitation' evokes the formal field of meteorology, while one would talk of 'rain' or 'rainfall' in describing the climate of one's country in a non-specialist context; that the multi-word unit 'see you!' is inappropriate as a parting remark by a student in a relationship of formality with, say, a university professor, or that 'in summary' is more appropriate as a phrase to conclude a piece of formal writing, rather than an informal phone-chat or a friendly personal letter.

▶   **TASK 81**

The following extract from Rudzka *et al.* (1981) gives register-related information for a set of six words all meaning, roughly, 'to complain'. Evaluate the relative merits of the scale of formality and the contextualized examples as ways of helping learners to become aware of how the words in different registers are used. Are the two modes of presentation inseparable? Would either be sufficient on its own?

All the words, except **complain**, are colloquial or informal and express irritation with the complainer. That is why **bellyache, grouse, grumble, moan** and **whine** are usually said of others and not of oneself.

The following scale shows how formal and informal they are:

formal	informal	colloquial		slang

←——

complain	**complain**	**grumble**	**grouse**	**moan**	**bellyache**
		whine			

The verbs can all appear in the construction **to** . . . . . **(to sb) about sth.**

EXAMPLES

complain   I **complained** to the airline about the loss of my luggage but they couldn't help me.

bellyache   Don't **bellyache** to me because there's no food left – you are an hour late for supper.
She is always **bellyaching** about the house being untidy but she never does anything about it.

grouse   He is always **grousing** to everyone about how he is overworked and underpaid.

grumble   Don't **grumble** to me about the people next door – go and complain to them.

moan   Everybody is always **moaning** about the rising cost of living.
You are strict with the children, then they come **moaning** to me about it.

whine   'What's that noise?' 'The dogs are **whining** to come in.'
She came **whining** to me this afternoon that no-one sympathized with her and that she felt she did not fit in with the rest of the group.

(*Rudzka* et al. *1981:83–4*)

Teaching materials attempt to build an awareness of register in a variety of ways. Most materials avoid the simple labelling or tagging of words with descriptions such as *formal* or *informal*, and in general, this is wise. Apart from a relatively small number of words that can be reliably tagged as only appropriate in informal contexts (e.g. 'kids', 'chap'), or only normally used in written contexts (e.g. 'herewith', 'omnibus'), and clearly delimited technical vocabularies, words acquire registerial appropriacy only in context. Thus typical register exercises involve comparing texts or recognizing inappropriate lexis. Soars and Soars (1987) offer both kinds for upper-intermediate learners. In the activity overleaf, two texts in the same field but with different tenors are jumbled:

● **Writing**

Formal and informal letters

1 Here are two jumbled letters. One is written to a hotel, and the other to a friend.
Work in pairs.
Decide which sentences go with which letter, and put them in the right order.

a. I would like a single room with a shower.
b. I'm writing to ask you a favour.
c. I don't mind where you put me. I'll sleep anywhere!
d. I have a further request.
e. I would like to make a reservation for the nights of 22nd, 23rd, and 24th January.
f. I hope the above is convenient.
g. Write soon and let me know.
h. I'm coming down to London at the end of the month to go to a conference.
i. Could I have a bite to eat when I arrive?
j. I hope you are all well, and that you've recovered from the busy Christmas period.
k. I would be extremely grateful.
l. Could I possibly have a room at the back, as I find front rooms rather noisy?
m. Could you put me up for a few days?
n. Just a sandwich will do.
o. I look forward to your reply.
p. It's the 22nd–24th January.
q. As I will be arriving quite late, could you possibly put a cold buffet in my room on the 22nd?
r. I hope that's all right.
s. There's something else I'd like to ask you.

(*Soars and Soars 1987:53*)

▶ TASK 82

Consider the Soars and Soars activity above from the point of view purely of *vocabulary* exploitation. How does vocabulary choice play a role in realizing register? Can you suggest a way in which the activity could involve the students in more *active* decisions on vocabulary choice for different registers?

In a follow-up activity, Soars and Soars suggest learners construct replies to the two jumbled letters, thus demanding a consistency of tenor between senders and receivers. Good register activities like these control the various dimensions of field, tenor and mode, and can be adapted to teaching aims. Other types of activity may depend on transferring one mode to another (e.g. informal speech to more formal writing).

▶ **TASK 83**

> Look back at the two Olympic boxing story texts in **4.4** (page 63) and consider ways in which the two texts might be used in class to illustrate the vocabulary differences.

It is not only along the parameter of tenor that register can be practised. Carter and Long (1987:94–108) offer a range of texts grouped according to subject-matter. But although the subjects may be similar, the texts display different *textual* structures (modes). Equally, texts of different lexical *density* (see **5.3**) will also be relevant to the study of register.

▶ **TASK 84**

> Consider how you might go about assembling a set of texts (written and spoken), displaying markedly different register characteristics, all on the subject of 'the weather'. What differences would you expect to find?

When it comes to discourse analysis and the types of phenomena observed in **4.3**, there are, as yet, no vocabulary materials which fully exploit the regularities of lexical patterning in discourse. Redman and Ellis (1989) present lower-intermediate level practice in lexical variation over sentence-boundaries in the exercise overleaf:

SEASIDE HOLS STILL TOPS

LAZING around on a beach is still the favourite holiday for Britons. And most of us prefer to do it at home, despite the popularity of foreign sun-spots.

According to a new Common Market survey, nearly 60 per cent of holidaying Britons head for the seaside and only a third of those go abroad.

Forty per cent of us take one holiday a year, but 21 per cent go away several times.

Last year 39 per cent didn't have a holiday at all, explaining that they couldn't afford one.

Stay

A third of those who went away chose to stay in hotels or guest houses. A fifth preferred to camp or caravan.

The *least* favourite holiday was the two-wheeled sort cycling or touring by motor-bike.

c We often repeat information in a text, but use different words and expressions to do so. For example, the idea of *tops* in the headline is repeated in the first sentence by the word *favourite*.

Find the words or expressions used in the text to repeat the following information also from the text.

First mention   →   second mention

	First mention	second mention
1	tops	favourite
2	foreign	....
3	sun-spots	....
4	head for	....
5	take a holiday	....
6	chose to	....

(*Redman and Ellis 1989:39*)

(For advanced-level examples, see McCarthy *et al.* 1985: 156.)

▶ TASK 85

Redman and Ellis's exercise is based on synonymy and paraphrase and is intended for lower-intermediate students. Can such discourse activities be introduced at lower levels and exploit the knowledge of basic synonyms that even quite elementary level learners have? What sorts of synonym pairs could be used? Construct a few example dialogues.

McCarthy (in press) discusses problems in the presentation of text-organizing words such as 'problem', 'issue', 'reason', and 'solution', but no materials as yet seem to have fully faced up to the difficulties of explaining these abstract words or of training learners to use them efficiently as textual signals. Teachers wishing to make their own materials are referred to Jordan's (1984) collection of English texts and the useful vocabulary reference lists that accompany them.

The insights of discourse analysis have yet to influence vocabulary teaching significantly, not least because the study of lexis in discourse has hardly begun on any serious scale. But many good materials already exist that stress differences between speech and writing, concentrating on both registerial factors and features of discourse.

▶ **TASK 86**

Examine the teaching materials you use, and identify exercises and activities that exploit either register or discourse features, even if this is not explicitly stated. Can the vocabulary element of such exercises be exploited to reinforce awareness of register and discourse?

8 Presenting vocabulary in the classroom

In this section, we move from preoccupations about the selection and organization of vocabulary for teaching to what actually happens in language classrooms. We shall look at the classroom mostly from the teacher's viewpoint, examining the ways in which the teacher introduces and explains vocabulary, and what sorts of decisions are involved. In 9 we will turn the spotlight more on the learner, and how learners interact with the teacher and other learners in the process of assimilating vocabulary. There we shall also consider the learner's individual strategies for learning and using vocabulary.

8.1 Pre-teaching

Most teachers accept that some sort of preparation for the introduction of new words in a lesson is a good idea. This corresponds not only to a practical need for some sort of focus and formalization to the content of the lesson, but also to a sound theoretical standpoint which says that new knowledge is most efficiently absorbed when it is assimilated to the already known, and when the appropriate conceptual frameworks or schemata are activated in the mind of the learner (see 3.4). Schemata are structured frameworks of knowledge, about the world and about language, in relation to which new information may or may not be perceived to make sense by the receiver. Schema theory is well-established in models of efficient reading (Carrell and Eisterhold 1983; Carrell 1987), but it is equally important in the classroom setting when the teacher is trying to activate existing knowledge to make the encounter with new words more meaningful.

A typical individual in modern society will have, for example, a schema associated with the notion 'holiday'; it will include settings and locations, probably the idea of travel, the notion of personal choice, rest, and recuperation, and so on. It will include typical sequences of actions, such as examining options, deciding, booking, making preparations, departing, and returning. The teacher can activate these notions, provide the essential vocabulary for them, and discover gaps in the learner's knowledge (either world or linguistic). This is a typical form of pre-teaching of vocabulary before, say, reading a text or listening to a tape on a new subject.

► TASK 87

What sort of schema do you have for the word 'marriage'? Consider such things as settings, participants, sequences of events, and so on. List the most important features of the schema.

If we were to compare schemata for 'marriage' for people from different cultures, we may well find variations; for 'holiday' too, there may be such variations; for some, 'holiday' will be closely bound up with the idea of religious festivals. So schema-activating often raises interesting aspects of the cultural contexts of words too. A typical schema-activation technique is for the teacher to ask a series of questions, for example, on the subject 'holidays':

'When you want to decide on a holiday, what do you read—travel brochures/advertisements? What will you want to read about in the brochures—cost/hotels/facilities/resorts? What will you do when you have decided—book/contact a travel agent/make reservations?'

The technique is straightforward and can evoke in the learner the vital feeling of 'need' for a word to fit a meaning that has been activated in the mind.

► TASK 88

What sort of schema-activating questions might you ask a group of learners if you wanted to pre-teach vocabulary on the subject of 'traffic problems'? What words do you predict would be needed to attach to the typical schemata of learners in an urbanized society?

Of course, pre-teaching does not have to depend on schema-activation. Words can be presented prior to their being encountered in their main context in a variety of ways.

Not all material is geared to pre-teaching. Seal's (1987) *Vocabulary Builder 1* stresses that the learner should engage actively in working out the meanings of new words encountered and that the teacher should therefore keep pre-teaching to a minimum, only asking 'a few brief pre-questions relating to the topic' (p. 6). Any direct pre-teaching of words should only be to help students understand the text; the key words indicated by the author, that is, the target words for which the text is presented, should not be pre-taught.

► TASK 89

Consider Seal's argument and place it against the standpoint that stresses schema-activation and pre-teaching of words. Both seem to stress active mental participation by the learner, but in different ways. Are the two incompatible? Under what circumstances might one line of argument rather than the other be followed?

Widdowson (1978:82–8) makes a distinction between two types of assistance the learner might be given to help with difficult vocabulary, termed *priming glossaries* and *prompting glossaries*. Priming glossaries, usually found at the beginning of reading passages, anticipate problems the learner will have, and sometimes deal with these problems by giving basic definitions of difficult words (what Widdowson calls the *signification* of the word). Alternatively, the priming glossary may give information as to the *value* of the word in its particular context (for a similar distinction, see Carter and McCarthy 1988, Chapter 5). Prompting glossaries usually appear after the passage and tend to give assistance with difficult words within the context of longer stretches of the text in question, in other words, they stress value rather than signification.

Both types of glossaries are useful, but Widdowson sounds a word of warning on prompting glossaries, insomuch as the learner's attention may be directed solely at working out the problems of a particular passage, at the expense of 'an interpreting strategy which can be applied generally to other discourse, when there will be no prompting glossary to assist' (p. 88).

8.2   Form and meaning

It was suggested in 3.2 that words may be stored mentally as much in terms of their phonological or graphological *form* as in terms of meaning, and so it should not be assumed that starting with a set of meanings and then proceeding to actual forms is the only valid way of presenting vocabulary. We have already seen in 7.3 how word-formation principles may be utilized in vocabulary materials, but grouping words together on the basis of other types of similarity, phonological and graphological, may also have advantages as input that can be easily assimilated.

Form

Henning (1973) suggests that lower level learners may particularly benefit from perceiving acoustic and orthographic similarities in words (see also Donley 1974). Redman and Ellis (*A Way with Words, Book 2*, 1990) encourage the learning of words in trios that have the same stress pattern and which rhyme.

---

a   The words below are all two-syllable verbs with the stress on the second syllable. For each one find two other verbs which rhyme with the second syllable.

Example:
repair   despair   compare

reduce   reply   retain   reform   respect   remand

b   [cassette] Listen to the cassette and check your answers. Write down any words from the recording which are not on your list.

(*Redman and Ellis 1990:106*)

Laufer (1981) raises the problem of words that have similar sounds but quite different meanings, which are frequently confused. These are referred to as *synophones*. English examples are 'sample'/'simple', 'cute'/'acute', 'affluence'/'influence'. The teacher may make a conscious decision to present such words together even if they might never otherwise crop up together in context, in the anticipation of problems arising from storage according to phonological or graphological cues. *Problems.*

▶ **TASK 90**

Suggest some synophones for the following words that might cause problems of recall due to similar sound patterns and/or rhymes:

wonder   e.g. *wander*
wink
scrape
croak
kitchen

It may not always be easy to predict synophones, but experienced language teachers become familiar with the same ones that crop up time and time again (e.g. 'wink' and 'blink', and the curious reversal of sounds in 'kitchen' and 'chicken'). Zimmerman (1987) found evidence of errors produced by sound-confusion with advanced German learners of English: the German '*schrammte*' (which should have translated as 'scraped'/ 'brushed alongside', or something similar) was translated variously as 'scrammed', 'scrabbed', and 'scratched'.

Meaning
However, most of the time, meaning will be the organizing principle of most vocabulary learning, and the teacher will proceed to explain the meanings of words in a way that (1) solves the immediate problems of comprehension for the learners and (2) enables them to relate the new word to words already known.

Words may be presented in or out of context. As we have seen, methods such as grids and networks (see 7.2) do not rely on context to establish meaning, and, even where words crop up in context, the teacher may deliberately *de-contextualize* them temporarily in order to get at general meaning, only to re-contextualize them later.

▶ **TASK 91**

Think of as many different ways as possible that you might explain to someone the meaning of the word 'mouth-organ', assuming you did not have one present (e.g. one way would be a definition).

Task 91 raises many possibilities: a picture (either drawn or ready-made), miming with hands to the mouth as if playing the instrument, or playing a tape-recording of a mouth-organ. Most teachers also have recourse to a variety of strictly linguistic methods:

1 definition: 'A mouth-organ is a musical instrument played by blowing . . .'
2 illustration/exemplification: 'Sometimes we see old men in the streets, poor men, beggars, playing the mouth-organ and asking for money.'
3 synonymy: 'Another word for "mouth-organ" is "harmonica".'
4 hyponymy: 'A mouth-organ is a type of small musical instrument.'

The explanation may be a combination of these types or may exploit antonyms or, where possible, direct translation to the students' L1.

▶   ## TASK 92

Consider these data extracts from Pender's (1988) study of vocabulary explanation in a Mexican classroom and classify the teacher's strategies for getting at meaning in terms of types 1 to 4 above:

1 (keyword: 'tycoon')
   T: JR in *Dallas*. He's a tycoon. Yes. He's very rich. He's got a lot of money. He's got a lot of influence and a lot of power

2 (keyword: 'slow down')
   S: What is slow down?
   T: Well what's slow
   S: Er (. . .)
   T: Yeah. It's the opposite of what?
   S: Fast

3 (keyword: 'alter')
   T: What do you think we might be able to substitute?
   S: Change
   T: Yeah, change, good

Notice that the teacher not only illustrates in the case of 'tycoon', but adds more and more characteristic features to the word (e.g. 'money', 'influence', 'power'). Furthermore, in 2 and 3 it is clear that the teacher is trying to instil in the students the practice of asking themselves the question 'What are the possible antonyms/synonyms of this word?', a learning skill that will be applicable to a vast number of other words.

Meaning to word: word to meaning
The teacher may introduce a word either by developing the meaning and then supplying the word, or alternatively, by presenting the word and then

developing its meaning. Taylor's (1986) data contains frequent examples of both methods:

(keyword: 'boots')
T: What do you call the special big shoes that come up to here, for when it's snowing?
S: Er . . .
T: Not shoes, but . . .

(keyword: 'in fact')
T: In fact, do you know what that means?
S: In fact.
T: In fact. Really.

Taylor found that for spoken contexts in which words were presented, the two methods, meaning to word and word to meaning, were both used, while word to meaning accounted for the majority of written contexts (1986:25–7).

► ## TASK 93

Look at these extracts from Taylor's data and identify the techniques used by the teacher to explain meaning. Consider also whether word to meaning or meaning to word is being used:

1 T: Can you tell me what detached means (points to picture)
  S1: What detached mean?
  T: Detached, yes
  S1: What is what
  T: It means . . . ask me . . . it means alone, not joined together
  S1: Siprate
  T: Now they are together . . . detached, together [mime]
  S1: Siprait, no?
  T: Separate. Separate, absolutely, separate?
  S1/S2: Separate

2 T: And we're going to see this. Where . . . what is the place where you go to listen to music or watch . . .
  S1: Cinema, cinema
  T: Actors
  S2: Not cinema
  T: Cinema is for film
  S1: Mm
  S2: Film
  T: But this is live, people on the stage acting
  S2: Party
  T: Yes, no
  S3: Not party
  T: It's not a party, it's a . . .

S3: (Arabic for 'theatre')
T: Theatre
S3: Theatre
T: Yes

What is notable in observing what teachers do to explain meaning is how they use a *variety* of strategies, usually more than just one, to explain a word. In the case of 'detached', synonymy ('alone', 'separate') and antonymy ('together') are both used, as well as mime. Further illustration is also used, especially where there is obviously confusion with another, related word ('theatre' and 'cinema'). In other words, teachers' strategies for explaining vocabulary may be seen as the discriminating use of the meaning relations we described in 2.3. Chaudron (1982) lists a wide range of such teacher strategies for elaborating vocabulary in the classroom. Even where meaning to word is the technique used, there will often be further explanation, either prompted by student uncertainty or simply because the teacher wishes to reinforce meaning, after the word has been produced. The 'theatre' extract continues:

S3: Theatre, theatre, is er for the singing?
T: Er sometimes singing, sometimes just acting . . . Shakespeare, er . . .
S3: Yeah

▶ **TASK 94**

Decide how you would develop the meanings of these words *before* actually presenting them, as with the 'theatre' example:

hire (a car)
put somebody up (for the night)
exhilarating
antique-shop

8.3 Types of stimuli

In most language courses the most frequent stimulus for the introduction of vocabulary is the written word, either in the form of words in contexts, or in lists or grids (see 7.2), but the written stimulus will usually be backed up by pronunciation practice and perhaps drilling of the word. It is usually the teacher who provides the acoustic backup to the written stimulus, though coursebooks may have accompanying tapes where vocabulary is introduced first through a listening activity (e.g. in the *A Way with Words* series by Redman and Ellis, 1989 and 1990). The interaction of spoken and written stimuli is apparent in this data extract from Taylor (1986:46), where a teacher and class are deciding what presents would be best for an imaginary set of characters, with the teacher holding up pictures of different items:

T: (Holding up a picture) What shall we give her?
S1: Oh (Arabic)
T: Mm . . . let's give her some . . .
S1: Pen, pen
T: Lipstick
S2: Lipstick
T: Pen for the lips, lipstick
S1: Lipstick
T: Let's give her some lipstick (writes on the board)
S1: Li . . . li . . . lipstick?
T: Lipstick, yes . . . let's give her a dishwasher . . . Now then (looking through pictures)
S3: /lɪbəstɪk/?
T: Lipstick
S3: Er . . . c . . . k?
T: That's right

For the students, the pronunciation and the spelling are both important stimuli. The initial stimulus here is a picture, and pictures are obviously a versatile resource for introducing new words; where real-life objects cannot be brought into the classroom, a picture often does the job and saves much laborious explanation. But pictures have their limitations too; not all words are easily explained by a visual stimulus, and visual stimuli can be misleading. A picture is a way of representing the *denotation* of the word (see 2.2); often it will only be possible to fully explain words through their sense relations with other words.

▶ TASK 95

Rank the following list of words in order of their amenability to explanation by using a picture. Where would you be most likely to find a picture for those you decide could be easily explained using a visual stimulus?

overcast	*accident*
stapler	*skirt*
fascinating	*painful*
greenhouse	*chimney*
however	*bumper*

Problem

Words that denote judgements, opinions, or evaluations—for example, the expressive and modal words described in 4.3, are perhaps least amenable to visual stimuli. In her excellent classroom data, Taylor (1986) has examples where visual stimuli are not wholly successful and considerable ambiguity exists as to the meaning of the word illustrated. A teacher uses a series of sports pictures to try to present the word 'interesting', but, as Taylor points out, the meaning transmitted could just as easily have been that of 'fast', 'stimulating', 'exhilarating', or several other words. The same difficulty would apply to words like 'fascinating' and 'painful' in Task 95.

8.4   Input, reinforcement, and uptake

Among the most difficult questions to answer concerning vocabulary teaching are: how much vocabulary should be introduced, how often does it need to be repeated, what are the best ways of committing new words to memory, and when can new vocabulary be said to be *learnt*?

Nation (1982) tries to answer some of these questions by synthesizing a wide range of research experiments. He concludes that learners *can* achieve extraordinary heights in memorizing words (as many as over 1,000 in 18 hours), but, at the other extreme, may also only achieve as few as 9 per hour (or 380 words in 42 hours). Initially, fast learners have a better chance of *retaining* the words they memorize than slower learners; as Nation puts it: 'fast learners are not fast forgetters'.

The method known as *suggestopedia* emphasizes memorization of vocabulary during sessions in which relaxation techniques play an important part. Learners sit in comfortable chairs with soft music playing in the background while the words are read aloud (for a good summary, see Richards and Rogers 1988). Some 1,500 words (150 new words per teaching unit) may be presented in 30 days during very intensive study sessions of 4 hours a day in a typical suggestopedia course. Proponents of the method claim that vast amounts of new vocabulary can be learnt in a very short time in this way, but at least one research experiment (Wagner and Tilney 1983) has suggested quite the opposite, with control-group subjects actually learning significantly *more* vocabulary in a 'traditional' classroom than experimental groups subjected to suggestopedic techniques.

▶ **TASK 96**

From the brief description of suggestopedia given above, do you think the method has something to offer? Is it your experience that learners learn more when they are physically and mentally relaxed? Are such relaxation techniques feasible in your teaching situation?

On the question of how many repetitions are necessary before a word can be memorized, it is apparent that some learners can learn words after only one encounter; seven repetitions seem to be enough for most people to be able to memorize a word (Nation 1982). Research seems to show that most forgetting occurs immediately after initial learning; this would seem to suggest that repetition is most effective if it commences very soon after the first encounter.

However, such figures and findings raise basic questions; recognition of words in tests is not the same as being able to recall a word, and even recalling a word in no way guarantees that one has mastered its use and 'knows' it in the fullest sense of the word (see Richards 1976 for a detailed specification of what it means to 'know' a word). What is more, learners who know they are going to be tested on a specific list of words use different techniques to learn than the learner who attends class every day and encounters new vocabulary via a wide range of stimuli. There is also the issue of receptive and productive knowledge of vocabulary as discussed in **3.2**. Nation (1982) reports one experiment that found the average number of encounters needed for most learners to recognize the meaning of a word was sixteen when students were not told they would be tested and did not consciously 'learn' the new vocabulary. Gairns and Redman (1986:66) suggest as few as eight to twelve new items may be appropriate (eight for elementary, twelve for advanced) per sixty-minute lesson for truly *productive* learning to take place.

Many of the encounters with new words which the average learner experiences are in written texts, and this raises the question of new-word density in texts (a subject not unconnected with lexical variation; see **5.3**). Nation (1982) reports on research which shows that, with short texts, a new-word density of up to one per 15 words of text does not impair learning. However, he does point out that even though abridged 'readers' for learners may stick to a target of one new word per 40 words of text, the length of the text could present a multitude of problems. There is, it would seem, an important balance to be struck between new-word density and length of text. New-word density will also be important when we consider the learner's ability to make intelligent guesses as to the meaning of new words (see **9.2**).

▶   TASK 97

Take any text that you have recently used, or are planning to use, in class with your learners and, from your knowledge of the students' vocabulary, do a new-word density count. Given its length, does the text, in your opinion, place an unduly light or heavy load of new words on your students, or is it about right?

When it comes to considering the best methods of effectively committing new vocabulary to memory, opinions and research findings vary again. Much has been made of the *keyword* technique, a technique whereby the subject makes a mental image that connects the new L2 word with an L1 word that has some formal (usually sound) association with the L2 word (Nation, ibid., provides a good summary of the method). For example, if the target word was the Malay word '*lorong*' (meaning a 'lane' in English), I might associate its sound pattern with the English word 'along', and visualize someone walking 'along' a lane:

It is claimed that this method fixes words effectively in memory. Kelly (1986) underlines the claim that making such formal and semantic links between words is superior to rote learning, and the method certainly seems to be powerful, if laborious. The main criticism against it is that one cannot possibly hope to perform the rather complex procedure on the hundreds of words that will have to be learnt and memorized if one is to come at all close to the target of a 2,000–3,000 word active vocabulary for learners mentioned by Færch *et al.* (1984:77).

Morgan and Rinvolucri (1986) use a variation on the keyword technique in an activity they call 'Pegwords'.

G/10 Pegwords

LEVEL   **Beginner to Advanced**

TIME   **10 minutes** at the start of the class and **5 minutes** at the end

IN CLASS   1 At the very start of your lesson, write the following on the board:

  one = bun   two = shoe   three = tree   four = door
  five = hive   six = sticks   seven = heaven   eight = gate
  nine = wine   ten = hen

2 Explain that you are going to show them a technique for remembering sequences of unrelated items. Each of the 'pegwords' above is associated (and rhymes) with an item's position in a list. They must then devise an image linking the 'pegword' and the item. For example, if item 8 was the word 'cat' then one might imagine a scene in which a cat was walking across the top of a field gate. The song 'Knick Knack Paddywhack' can be used to learn the 'pegwords'.

3 Write the word list on the blackboard. Number each item 1–10.

4 Ask the students, working individually, to imagine a scene or situation linking each word with its appropriate 'pegword'. Allow no writing.

5 Clean the blackboard, and get on with some other, unrelated piece of work.

6 At the end of the lesson, ask the students to write down the original list of words from memory, *in the correct sequence*.

Acknowledgement
We found this technique in A. Baddeley: *Your Memory* (Penguin 1983) and heard about its use in class from Antonia Paín of Caceres University.

(*Morgan and Rinvolucri 1986:118*)

▶ ## TASK 98

Try out your ability to make keyword associations as in the Malay example ('*lorong*') above, for these pairs of words. Remember the procedure:

1 Associate the spoken L2 word with an English word (the 'keyword') that sounds like the L2 word.

2 Form a mental image of the keyword interacting with the correct English translation.

L2 word	spoken pronunciation	English translation
allumette (French)	/æljumet/	match (to light)
ventana (Spanish)	/ventænæ/	window
smör (Swedish)	/smɜːr/	butter
dom (Russian)	/dɒm/	house

Methods like the keyword method and rote learning of lists presuppose the decontextualization of words, but it may be argued that the best way of assuring that a word is remembered and assimilated is by meeting it in some meaningful context. However, Nation (1982) argues that context may not necessarily be the most efficient way of getting the meaning of a word across, and in the early stages of language learning, a word and its translation may be a more effective stimulus. What is more, a good definition or explanation may obviate the need to present a word in the variety of contexts required to fully cover its meaning. Nation also makes two other points that cannot be ignored: word-*form* may be better remembered if the words are listed with their translations, and secondly, learning in context does not seem to prevent learners from translating the target word into their L1.

Effective memorizing and assimilation of words is probably not the result of any single method, and the good learner will operate a variety of techniques, some of which will be highly individual and idiosyncratic; indeed, encouraging learner autonomy (see **9.4**) in such matters is probably the best way to foster good vocabulary memorization.

9 Teachers and learners

In **8**, we concentrated on vocabulary presentation in the classroom very much from the teacher's point of view, but success in the vocabulary lesson crucially depends on the interaction between teacher and learners, and on the work the learners themselves put into the assimilation and practising of new words. Now we shall consider the mechanisms of teacher–learner interaction in the transmission of new words and new meanings, the strategies adopted by learners to achieve their goals in vocabulary learning, and the ways in which they put their limited lexical resources to use.

9.1 Classroom interaction

Both teachers and pupils have to work hard to 'construct' meaning (see **3.4**); meaning is not just lying on a plate, waiting to be picked up and instantly digested. The teacher has to present meaning in a way that is comprehensible to learners, and learners have to relate new meanings to ones already known. They should signal to the teacher if they feel that meaning cannot be grasped unless more information is given and, ideally, try out newly acquired words in class to provide feedback for both themselves and the teacher, who has to be reasonably confident that word and meaning have been successfully transmitted.

All of these mechanisms are apparent in classroom data; the vocabulary class is a place where meaning is *negotiated* between teacher and learner, on some occasions more successfully than others.

▶ TASK 99

> Discuss with other teachers ways in which students typically contribute towards the establishing of meaning of new words in interaction with the teacher. What sorts of questions do they ask? Do 'good' learners make different contributions from those of weaker pupils?
>
> Note down the results of your discussion.

Active learners seem to make similar contributions to those of teachers in classroom interaction; they attempt to organize new words in relation to words already known; they define and paraphrase words and try using words in examples. Note these examples from Pender's (1988) data, where students supply a definition and synonyms, and ask the teacher questions to get a more specific meaning:

1 T: Story and history, what's the difference?
   S: Story is a tale and history is the truth, something that happened in the past

2 T: Developments, any ideas how you could explain that, another word for development, or another way to say it
   S: To discover something
   T: To discover or to
   S: To invent

3 (The teacher is explaining 'check', as in 'check pattern'.)
   T: Red, white, red, white, red, white, then on the next line, white, red, white, red, white, red, it's
   S: It's always squares, always?
   T: They're squares if it's checked, they're squares, yeah. Why?
   S: Um, even if they're spots or something?
   T: No, if they're spots, then you would call it spotted . . .

In such interaction, teacher and pupils engage in a problem-solving activity together; motivation seems to be high on the part of the students to fix new words and their meanings, and acquisition could be enhanced by such interaction.

Core and procedural vocabulary in the classroom

Classroom data provides us with good examples of how students and teachers interact when new words and meanings are being discussed. Most notable is the role played by *core* vocabulary (see **4.1**) and *procedural* vocabulary (see **4.2**) as used by teachers and pupils. Note how in this example from Pender's (1988) data, core items ('spare time', 'free time') are used by the teacher and a student to establish the meaning of the non-core 'leisure':

T: Leisure is what?
S: Spare time
S: Leisure are some activities that we do with leisure, no? For example, for use, for example, for me dancing is a leisure activity, no?
T: Well it would be. It would be an activity that you do in your leisure time or your free time at your leisure
S: And that you like, no?
T: Well, when you speak of leisure you're, you're speaking of free time away from your work, when you want to do something that you like
    . . .

The use of procedural vocabulary is fundamental to the strategies of definition and paraphrase; procedural (or highly indexical) words establish basic cognitive categories for words (type, size, colour, material, dimensions, intensity, etc.), and those used in dictionaries for this purpose are also found in the class; two further examples from Pender's data illustrate the teacher using procedural words, to explain 'laces' and 'lining':

('laces')
T: Tennis shoes have laces. What are laces?
S: These . . . you fasten on something
T: Yes, two little pieces of material that you have to put through your shoe and then tie at the end in order to keep your shoes on. Right, okay

('lining')
S: What's lining?
T: Lining. Lining is when you have um you have er a jacket or a coat and inside there's another kind of material, kind of soft, sometimes shiny inside. Do you have a lining inside your jacket, yeah, what's it's (shows lining of jacket)
S: Forro
T: Yeah, right. The red, the red material is the lining in his jacket

Taylor (1986:12ff.) points out that a good deal of vocabulary which is not necessarily of high frequency outside the classroom occurs frequently in the classroom in a procedural role (see **4.2**). The meaning of such vocabulary is assumed, and it operates as the basis of negotiation of meaning. Words such as 'call', 'find', 'special', and, in the examples above, 'material', 'kind', 'in order to', are very frequent in vocabulary explanation. Interestingly enough, they may not necessarily occur in the coursebook as words to be taught; they seem to be assimilated simply by frequent encounter, and are used by teachers and pupils alike.

▶ TASK 100

Look at these extracts from Pender's data and note occurrences of core and procedural vocabulary. Note especially words which would not normally be considered as words of very high frequency outside the classroom; note also who uses which words, teacher or student:

1 T: How about, um, four, four is what?
   S: Knife
   T: Knives
   S: Kitchen knife
   T: Well, kitchen knife would be
   S: Bre, bread knife
   T: Okay, it's a bread knife. Kitchen knives wouldn't be specific

enough, they could be different shapes and sizes. Okay, there's a bread knife. Does anybody know another word for the bread knife? Do you know which is the bread knife?

S: Yes, yes

T: The big one. Okay, what's another word that you could use for that? Anybody? You could also call it a carving, a carving knife. Do you know what carving means?

S: Carving means to cut

T: Okay, yeah, if you have a turkey especially, um or a big piece of meat and someone is going to cut you could say 'would you please carve the turkey?' It means to cut into special pieces

S: To slice

T: To cut into pieces, slice it . . .

2 T: What part of the tree do you think a branch is?

S: Small . . . smaller trees

T: Not a small tree as such, imagine you've got a big tree. What part of the tree is the branch?

S: The part where the leaves come, come in, come out

T: Yeah, the part where the leaves grow . . .

3 T: Epaulets, it's a piece of material like a little strip with maybe a button or a strap

S: We don't have a special name for that, we call maybe hombreras but now we are calling that the thick thing that . . .

T: Well, this is not an exceptionally common word, it's only used for this, . . .

9.2 Learning strategies

Learners adopt a number of strategies for coping with new vocabulary, but not all learners are equally good at maximizing their strategic resources. Medani (1989) studied the vocabulary learning strategies of both good and poor (in the sense of under-achieving) Arabic learners of English, and found considerable variation in what successful learners did and what the under-achievers did. He studied a wide range of strategies, including what students did to memorize words, how they used dictionaries, how they used the teacher as informant, how they practised using new words, and how they took notes. His subjects used both bilingual and monolingual dictionaries (see 10.1), made notes of some sort on new words, and used a variety of memorization techniques.

▶ TASK 101

Here are some of Medani's statistics for sources used by his subjects to get information about difficult words on first encounter. The figures show the frequency of occurrence of each strategy in his data. How far do these statistics correspond to intuitive feelings that you have as to how your own students behave: Would you expect your students to produce a similar set of relative differences if they were the subjects of an investigation like this one?

		occurrences
1	Ask classmates	229
2	Guessing	215
3	Ask teacher	170
4	Overlook	103
5	Ask about meaning by demanding English paraphrase or synonym	81
6	Ask for Arabic equivalent	79
7	Ask for a sentence showing word usage	59
8	Group work	100
9	Dictionary	192

Medani's study is of great value because he not only considered *good* learners; he also separated his statistics to show the relative differences for the given strategies between the good and poor learners. For instance, the poor learners seemed to *practise* new words considerably less than the good ones. The latter regularly tried out new words when opportunities arose (e.g. writing compositions), asked questions to confirm their knowledge, and tested themselves by going through word lists.

Guessing and inferring meaning *in reading*
Among the most common strategies that students employ are making guesses and inferences about new words. Inferring involves creating a schema (see **3.4**) for the unknown word(s), based on world knowledge and previous experience, both of the world and texts; it means drawing conclusions as to word meaning by following certain rational steps in the face of the evidence available. If, for instance, a learner is faced with the sentence 'There are a lot of nasty snags yet to overcome' (taken from a British newspaper) and does not know what 'nasty snags' means, then, apart from the general context (in this case an article about progress in East–West disarmament talks), it is possible to infer that 'snags' is a countable noun, that they are something which can be 'overcome', and therefore, given the subject-matter, may mean something like 'problems', or 'obstacles', or 'difficulties', which can also be 'overcome'. If they are 'problems', then 'nasty' is not likely to mean something positive like 'good' or 'wonderful', though it could mean something like 'small' or 'minor', and so on. Inferring in this way is an example of the *construction* of meaning by the reader/listener, as was described in **3.4**. It is the process we might hope the good learner would follow when faced with difficulty in reading, or during a test, or any situation where running to the dictionary or asking someone was not possible or appropriate.

► ## TASK 102

Consider possible ways in which the teacher might help students develop their inference skills by activities in the classroom. Draw up a list of important things that learners should do when inferring the meaning of new words in a reading text (e.g. look for morphological clues as to word-class; decide whether the item is subject, verb, or object, of its clause). If possible, compare your list with others'.

One suggestion, by Færch *et al.* (1984:96) is that 'think-aloud' sessions are a good idea to train inference skills; the learner relates out loud the step-by-step process he or she goes through in inferring meaning.

Brutten (1981) suggests that teachers are very good at predicting the words learners will have difficulties with; Brutten also suggests that students are surprisingly good on some occasions at guessing words even when they are of low frequency; much depends on the text in which the words are included.

Liu and Nation (1985) studied learners' ability to guess the meaning of nonsense words used to replace real words at regular intervals in written texts. Guesses were to be made using contextual clues. They found that success depended on the relative density of unknown words. Where there was only one nonsense word per twenty-five words, they were easier to guess than when there was one every ten words. Their texts with invented words were in some way a mirror of the lexical variation discussed in 5.3; the higher the variation the more difficult the text is likely to be for the learner, and guessing will become harder. Liu and Nation's high-density text began like this:

'*The Origins of Economics*
While man's feldination about his material alamution can be prined to ancient times, the development of prinavalic economics is of relatively recent origin.'

► ## TASK 103

Test your own ability to make sense of the nonsense words in Liu and Nation's text. Do you think nonsense words are a good technique for encouraging inference and guessing skills, or should one always use real words?

Xiaolong's (1988) research suggests that those learners who are good at word inference also *retain* the first-encounter contextual meaning of the target words better. Xiaolong concludes that there is a link between recalling words and the contexts in which they were learnt.

One task for the vocabulary teacher in the continuous evaluation of success (or lack of it) in the vocabulary teaching and learning enterprise will be to monitor learners' use of inferencing skills. Such skills may come naturally to many learners, but some learners may lack them, or misdirect them, or be accustomed to learning modes where such skills are not developed or encouraged, in which case direct teaching and practising of the skills may be needed.

9.3 Note-taking

Keeping some sort of written record of new vocabulary is quite an important part of language learning for many students. The very act of writing a word down often helps to fix it in the memory, even if only with regard to its spelling. Written records can take a variety of forms: card-index files are one; they are flexible as far as the amount of information recorded on each card is concerned; they can be flicked through for alphabetical searching or just 'browsed' in and, most usefully of all, they can be *re*arranged as the user perceives new possible groupings and associations between words.

▶ TASK 104

Draw up a list of possible strategies which you think students might use for noting vocabulary during a lesson (for example, an L1 translation, or a drawing). If you can, compare your list with someone else's and decide which strategies you think are likely to be most common.

The vocabulary notebook is probably the most common form of written student record. Small notebooks can be carried round easily and added to and studied at any time. When we look at typical student notebooks, though, we find a variety of types of entry, and some books look much better organized than others. Particular sections of the notebook tell us a lot about what has gone on in class or in the course material. Sometimes a clear formal or semantic grouping can be perceived; at other times students just seem to enter words that have cropped up.

Compare these two authentic extracts from a student's notebook:

1 to give up = cut down (my smoking)
  to take down a book
  to pick up a book

2 fled – go away / waist start to spread – dead – gobble up (eat very quickly) – gob = mouth – to nod off – (I nodded off on the underground)

Both extracts are from the same student's book. The first is clearly concerned with occurrences of 'down' and 'up' in phrasal verbs. The second is a more loosely connected list which may have made more sense in the context of the lesson itself. The student uses the 'equals' (=) sign to indicate synonymy ('gob' = 'mouth') but it is not clear whether (s)he thinks 'give up' and 'cut down' are synonymous or just closely associated words. Bracketed matter seems to indicate examples or paraphrase.

► ## TASK 105

Look at these extracts from student notebooks and consider what strategies the students have used. Which student seems best organized and for what reasons? Do you think the best organized notebook will necessarily lead to the most efficient learning? Can you account for errors in transcription?

spend	–	verbringen
move	–	verlegen bewege
fogee	–	schlechte sicht
Eici	–	Eisig
icy		
corner	–	kurve
quiet fast	–	bischa schnell
eastemeit	–	ungefahr
estimate		

by land	by air	by water
a moped	an airship	a submarine
a van	a rocket	a canoe
a jeep	a helicopter	a rowing boat
a train	a jet	a barge
a double decker	a glider	a liner
	a hot air balloon	

Teachers can learn a lot by occasionally looking at learners' written records: persistent problems with spelling/transcription, mistranslations, over-reliance on translation, and use of a range of recording strategies can all act as important feedback on the lesson and on the performance and progress of individuals.

Redman and Ellis believe that students should be explicitly encouraged in good note-taking habits, and include a practical exercise on different note-taking strategies in their book *A Way with Words* (1989:3–4). The authors find (personal communication) that decisions on the best strategy in individual cases are often culturally motivated, depending not only on whether the L2 word can be related to an L1 word, but whether the L2 meaning can be readily conceptualized or not in the learner's cultural experience from L1.

Student notebooks offer a fascinating insight into the individual learning styles that may be present in groups, and can alert the teacher to learning problems which might not otherwise be so clearly revealed.

9.4 Learner autonomy

Recently, attention has turned to ways in which learners can be trained to take more responsibility for how and what they learn, and organizing vocabulary learning is a particularly productive area for the encouragement of learner autonomy. New vocabulary materials (e.g. Redman and Ellis 1989, 1990) stress the role of the individual learner, and one book on learner autonomy (Ellis and Sinclair 1989) has a section devoted to vocabulary learning.

Ellis and Sinclair report a number of individual responses to the task of learning vocabulary by students of different levels and different mother tongues. We saw in **6.2** how particular words may be perceived as easy or difficult by individual learners, and in **9.3** we looked at individual ways in which learners go about recording the vocabulary they learn. Ellis and Sinclair's book is intended to encourage reflection by the learner on ways of learning and to develop individual approaches to solving problems. Learners are encouraged to ask themselves what is important for them to know about individual words, in relation to a check-list based on Richards' (1976) list of features of 'knowing' a word. They are also encouraged to assess their own vocabulary needs and shortcomings regularly, and to keep a record of their performance in actual situations. Two students, Stig and Mimi, assessed themselves as follows:

Name: *Stig*

Date	Activity/Situation	Points to assess	Assessment
26.7.88	*Testing vocabulary on washing machines for writing instructions*	*– spelling* *– labelling parts of* * machine correctly*	*Poor!* *Need more specific vocabulary.*

Name: *Mimi*

Date	Activity/Situation	Points to assess	Assessment
26.7.88	*Talking to Fred about nuclear accidents*	*Vocabulary*	*OK but:* *– polite ways of interrupting* *– special vocabulary for* * nuclear accidents*

(*Ellis and Sinclair 1989:32*)

The assessment then leads to a personal programme for remedying any shortcomings the students perceive in their own performance.

Learners can also be encouraged to develop their own personal learning styles for vocabulary, in such areas as memorizing and retaining new words. Research has shown (Atkinson 1972) that learners who controlled how they learnt words performed 50 per cent better in retention tests than when they had to study random word lists set for them. Control might simply be some individual way of recording words or of testing oneself over periods of time, or it may be a case of making highly idiosyncratic associations for new words not necessarily in line with their semantic composition or their place in lexical fields (see 2.2 and 2.3). Morgan and Rinvolucri suggest activities to foster such idiosyncratic associations: students are asked to categorize a given list of words under headings such as 'nice' words and 'nasty' words, or to associate words with shapes such as circles and triangles, and to justify their individual choices (Morgan and Rinvolucri 1986:109–10). Ellis and Sinclair (1989) see a word network of the type illustrated opposite as a useful way for the learner to record personal associations of a word (see also the encyclopaedic network on page 41, which attempts to represent the individual's personal knowledge of a word in the typical L1 context). Their example is a network for 'politics':

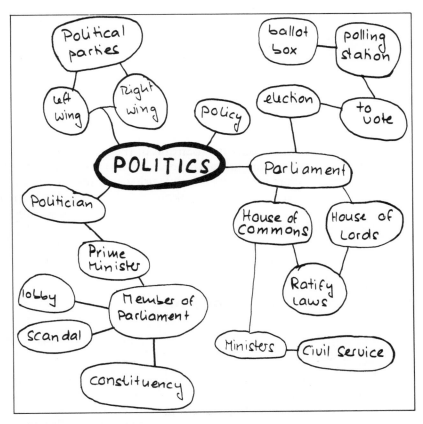

(*Ellis and Sinclair 1989:36*)

▶ ## TASK 106

1 Draw up a random list of fifteen to twenty words and try to categorize them under different headings according to personal preferences (for instance, you might categorize them under two headings: 'hot' and 'cold' words, or 'boring' and 'interesting' words). Compare your list and its groupings with someone else's.

2 Have you ever developed any other individual ways of learning new words in foreign languages? Do any of the ways resemble those discussed and illustrated above?

10   Lexical reference

Recent years have seen an expansion in the available resources of lexical reference aimed at language learners. The learner looking to obtain useful vocabulary reference books is faced with an array of learner's dictionaries, lexicons, and thesauruses all making claims to provide learners with the information they need in an accessible form. In this section we consider types of reference works, their advantages and disadvantages, and then look at workbooks and activities built around the skills needed to use such works effectively.

10.1 Types of reference book

Dictionaries
For our purposes, the two kinds of dictionary that most concern us are monolingual learner's dictionaries and bilingual dictionaries.

Monolingual learner's dictionaries have made considerable progress since the first (1948) edition of Hornby's *Oxford Advanced Learner's Dictionary of Current English* (*OALDCE*). In addition to the latest, updated (1989) edition of this pioneering work there are the *Longman Dictionary of Contemporary English* (*LDOCE*) (latest edition 1987) and the *Collins-COBUILD English Language Dictionary* (1987). All three offer detailed information about their many thousands of headwords, which are arranged alphabetically. There are differences in these three major dictionaries and, as Nesi (1988) points out, choosing the best one is very difficult, and depends on individual needs.

► TASK 107

Consider these three entries for the word 'interfere'. What are the principal differences, if any, in (a) amount of information; (b) types of information; (c) the language used to explain the word, and (d) symbols and other graphic conventions?

in·ter·fere /ˌɪntəˈfɪə(r)/ *v* **1** [I, Ipr] ~ **(in sth)**; ~ **(between sb and sb)** concern oneself with or take action affecting sb else's affairs without the right to do so or being invited to do so: *Don't interfere in matters that do not concern you!* ○ *It's unwise to interfere between husband and wife.* **2** [Ipr] ~ **with sth** (**a**) handle, adjust, etc sth without permission, esp so as to cause damage: *Who's been interfering with the clock? It's stopped.* (**b**) obstruct sth wholly or partially; prevent sth from being done or carried out properly: *interfere with sb else's plans* ○ *Don't allow pleasure to interfere with duty.* **3** [Ipr] ~ **with sb** (**a**) distract or hinder sb: *Don't interfere with him while he's working.* (**b**) (*Brit euph*) assault sb sexually: *The police reported that the murdered child had not been interfered with.*
▷ **in·ter·fer·ence** /ˌɪntəˈfɪərəns/ *n* [U] **1** ~ **(in/ with sth)** interfering: *I don't want any interference from you!* **2** (**a**) (*radio*) prevention of clear reception because a second signal is being transmitted on a wavelength close to the first: *interference from foreign broadcasting stations.* (**b**) (*computing*) presence of unwanted signals in a communications circuit. (**c**) (*sport esp US*) (in ice hockey, American football, etc) unlawful obstruction of an opposing player.
in·ter·fer·ing *adj* [attrib] likely to concern oneself annoyingly with other people's affairs, to try to control what they do, etc: *She's an interfering old busybody!*

1 (*OALDCE* 1989)

interfere /ɪntəfɪə/, **interferes, interfering, interfered.** **1** If you **interfere** in a relationship or situation between people, you try to influence it, especially when there is a dispute and you aim to solve the problem; often used showing disapproval. ᴇɢ *He has instructed his family not to interfere... My mother interferes in things... They didn't interfere with us and we didn't interfere with them... It is sometimes dangerous to interfere between parents and children.* `V : IF · PREP THEN in with between = meddle`
2 If you **interfere** in a conversation between other people, you interrupt them when their conversation does not concern you; used showing disapproval. ᴇɢ *Please don't interfere, Boris. This is very important... Don't let me interfere.* `V : IF+PREP THEN in = butt in`
3 Something that **interferes** with a situation or activity has a damaging effect on it, often preventing something from happening or succeeding; used showing disapproval. ᴇɢ *Child-bearing will not interfere with a career... She has done nothing that directly interfered with the actions of the others... The clock was stopped from striking because it interfered with the performances.* `V : IF+PREP THEN with = conflict, clash`
4 When sounds or radio waves **interfere** with each other, they get too close to each other and become mixed up, so that people cannot hear them or receive them properly. ᴇɢ *Why did their calls not interfere with one another, jamming the signals?... There was evidence of pirate radios interfering with shipping.* `V+A (with)`
5 Someone who **interferes** with a child behaves in a sexual way towards him or her; used showing disapproval. ᴇɢ *They were interfered with by their babysitter.* `V+A (with)`

2 (*LDOCE* 1987)

in·ter·fere /ˌɪntəˈfɪəʳ‖-tər-/ *v* [I (**in, between**)] *derog* to enter into or take part in a matter which does not concern one, and in which one is not wanted: *I never interfere between husband and wife|in other people's affairs.|He's just an interfering old busybody.*
interfere with sbdy./sthg. *phr v* [T] **1** to get in the way of; prevent from working or happening: *The sound of the radio upstairs interferes with my work.* **2** to touch or move (something) in a way that is annoying or not allowed: *Who's been interfering with my books?* **3** *euph* to touch or annoy (someone) sexually: *He got put in prison for interfering with little girls.*

3 (*COBUILD* 1987)

Not least, the dictionary entries in Task 107 vary as to what the learner is told about pronunciation. All three use IPA (International Phonetic Alphabet) symbols; the learner who cannot read these is at a complete loss, and the ability to interpret IPA symbols may have to be taught directly and practised in class if efficient dictionary use is to be fostered. The *COBUILD* dictionary especially goes to even greater lengths, and by using bold face and superscripts, indicates syllables that may bear main stresses and a range of possible pronunciations for weak syllables: 'financial' is indicated as /fɪ^{5}nænʃə^{0}l/, telling the user that the /ɪ/ may have a pronunciation ranging from /ə/ to /aɪ/, while the ə^0 indicates a range from /ə/ to no realization at all. This is an innovative attempt at capturing the variation found in real speech, but it depends crucially on the user's willingness to learn a complex notation, or at least to refer to the front-matter, to solve pronunciation difficulties, and to get the fullest information.

On the question of effectiveness of explanation of *meaning*, the ideal learner's dictionary should give a sufficiently clear explanation not only for the learner to *decode* meaning but also to *encode* without error. This is probably an impossible task, and current learners' dictionaries cannot offer 100 per cent guarantees against error. It is interesting to compare the ability of learners' dictionaries to help learners avoid classic, recurring errors or errors between words close in form and/or meaning. One of the attested learner errors of collocation cited in **2.1** was the learner who said 'you've "rescued" my life', instead of 'saved'. If we look at the *COBUILD* entries for 'save' and 'rescue', the entry for 'save' does indeed include a collocation with 'life' in an example, but it is not clear whether 'life' could be used with 'rescue'; both are given as transitive (V + O):

> **save** /seɪv/, **saves, saving, saved**. **1** If you **save**   V+O : IF+PREP
> someone or something, you help them to avoid harm   THEN *from*
> or failure or to escape from a dangerous or unpleas-   ⌃ rescue
> ant situation. EG *An artificial heart could save his*
> *life... They prayed for rain to save the starving*
> *village... She saved him from drowning... They were*
> *trying to save their marriage.* ● If you say that you   ● PHR : USED AS
> cannot do something to **save** your **life**, you mean   AN A
> that you cannot do it at all, no matter how hard you
> try; an informal expression. EG *I couldn't write a*
> *novel to save my life... He can't sing to save his life.*

> **rescue** /rɛskjuː/, **rescues, rescuing, rescued**.
> **1** If you **rescue** someone or something, you take   V+O
> action to help them get away from a dangerous or
> harmful situation. EG *All my attempts to rescue him*
> *were in vain... He was rescued from the sinking*
> *aircraft... The Cabinet decided on 3 February not to*
> *rescue the company.*
> **2 Rescue** is help which is given to someone or   N UNCOUNT
> something which saves them from a dangerous or   = deliverance
> unpleasant situation. EG *Rescue was at hand... You*
> *might dream of rescue, but it's useless.*
> **3** If you **go** or **come to the rescue** of someone or   PHR : VB
> something, you help them when they are in danger   INFLECTS
> or difficulty. EG *It was William who came to the*
> *rescue... Toby came to my rescue.*
> **3 A rescue** is a successful attempt to save someone   N COUNT
> or something from a difficult or dangerous situation.   ⌃ recovery
> EG *The coastguard may be working on as many as 20*
> *rescues at any one time.*

(*COBUILD 1987*)

Tomaszczyk (1981) has pointed out that *bilingual* dictionaries have tended in the past to try to cover too much, and to cater for everyone from scholars to ordinary learners, instead of orienting themselves to learners' basic needs. There has also been a tendency for L1-to-L2 dictionaries to function more as reading (decoding) dictionaries for L2 users rather than as productive (encoding) dictionaries for L1 users. There is no doubt that a new generation of bilingual reference works is long overdue to reflect progress and innovations in the world of EFL lexical reference.

Some dictionaries are specifically designed to help learners avoid error, most notably the *Longman Dictionary of Common Errors* (Heaton and Turton 1987). This dictionary is based on an analysis of a corpus of students' work and examination scripts and covers some 1,700 common errors with an example of each, a corrected version, and a short explanation. In the bilingual field, there have long existed dictionaries of cognate words (words in different languages sharing the same origin) and 'false friends' (words similar in form but different in meaning or usage in two languages). A recent example for Italian and English is Browne's *Odd Pairs and False Friends* (1987), where, instead of having to make two searches in separate parts of the dictionary, the false friends are brought together in paired entries. Here is a typical entry, for English 'impressed', and Italian '*impressionato*':

---

impressed *agg.* colpito favorevolmente *da qualcosa o qualcuno*: **they were impressed by the splendid new Parliament building; I was impressed by the young pianist at last night's concert.**

impressionato agg. ⬜1 (deeply) shocked: **l'opinione pubblica è rimasta profondamente impressionata dalla notizia dell'attentato**, public opinion was (deeply) shocked by the news of the bomb outrage. ⬜2 horrified: **rimasi impressionato dalle sue ferite**, I was horrified by his injuries. ⬜3 frightened, scared: **rimasero impressionati dalla violenza del temporale**, they were frightened (*o* scared) by the violence of the storm.

(*Browne 1987:122*)

Collocation in the dictionary
In 2.1 it was noted that collocational appropriacy was a problem for learners. Dictionaries vary in the quality of the information they give on collocations, and often the learner has to assume that the collocations which appear in the example sentences or phrases given are the most appropriate ones. The *BBI Combinatory Dictionary of English* (Benson, Benson, and Ilson 1986) sets out explicitly to give the most common collocations for its headwords. Definition is kept to an absolute minimum and entries concentrate on collocates.

▶ TASK 110

Before looking at the extracts from the *BBI* dictionary below, try to answer the following questions:

1 What adverb modifiers might precede the adjective *damaged*?
    (_____-ly damaged)
2 List some verbs that might occur with the noun 'a dance' (e.g. '*have* a dance').

Now compare your answers with the *BBI* dictionary:

damage I *n.* ['harm'] 1. to cause, do ~ to; to inflict ~ on 2. to suffer, sustain ~ 3. to repair, undo ~ 4. grave, great, extensive, irreparable, serious, severe; lasting, permanent; light, slight; widespread ~ 5. fire; flood; material; property; structural ~ 6. brain ~ (irreversible brain ~) 7. ~ from (~ from the fire) 8. ~ to (was there much ~ to the car? the ~ done to the house was extensive; grave ~ to one's reputation)
damage II *v.* 1. to ~ badly 2. easily ~d

dance I *n.* 1. to do, perform a ~ 2. to have a ~ with 3. to sit out a ~ 4. (the) classical ~; modern ~ 5. a barn; belly; circle, round; folk; formal; square; sword; tap; war ~ 6. to go to a ~ 7. at a ~ (they met at a ~) 8. (misc.) (BE) to lead smb. a merry ~ (AE has *to lead smb. a merry chase*)
dance II *v.* 1. (D; intr.) to ~ to (to ~ to the music of a rock group) 2. (D; intr.) to ~ with 3. (misc.) to ~ for, with joy

(*Benson, Benson, and Ilson 1986:66*)

Deciding on the best way to present collocational information in the dictionary is not an easy task. The *BBI* dictionary gives examples as illustrated in Task 110, but there are other possibilities, including a collocational dictionary using the grids that have been utilized in other types of vocabulary materials (see 7.2).

The authors of the *BBI* dictionary claim dramatic success for it in terms of enabling learners to encode appropriate collocations. In pre- and post-testing of groups of learners introduced to the *BBI* dictionary, scores increased, from a mean of 32 per cent and 43 per cent, to 93 per cent and 92 per cent respectively (Benson and Benson 1988).

▶ TASK 111

Think of possible ways of presenting collocational information in a dictionary or other types of reference work, either building on the grid method or the *BBI* style, or else in a completely different way. If possible, compare your results with other people's.

Lexicons and thesauruses
Alphabetical dictionaries are not the only, and not necessarily the best, way of arranging the words of a language. In **2.3** we saw how words cluster into lexical fields which realize semantic fields (i.e. the sub-divisions of the meaning potential of the language as a whole). Thesaurus-type books arrange their entries around such fields, the most famous thesaurus for

English being *Roget's Thesaurus*: it was first published in 1852, but has seen new editions and updatings since then (e.g. Kirkpatrick (ed.) 1987).

Roget's Thesaurus, however, was based on philosophical categories which may not have much psychological validity for the average language learner. Its purpose, too, was to enable writers to refine their choice of word, with synonyms and near-synonyms, or to make a more precise choice of vocabulary. Modern thesauruses (or *lexicons* as they are also sometimes called) aim more at giving the L1 user or learner of an L2 access to the vocabulary of a particular field in everyday contexts and topics. Thus the *Longman Lexicon of Contemporary English* (McArthur 1981) has, in marked contrast to the philosophical categories of Roget, a series of headings more attuned to pedagogical needs:

THE LEXICON

A	Life and Living Things	1	H	Substances, Materials, Objects, and Equipment	381
B	The Body; its Functions and Welfare	39	I	Arts and Crafts, Science and Technology, Industry and Education	429
C	People and the Family	79			
D	Buildings, Houses, the Home, Clothes, Belongings, and Personal Care	169	J	Numbers, Measurement, Money, and Commerce	457
E	Food, Drink, and Farming	213	K	Entertainment, Sports, and Games	505
F	Feelings, Emotions, Attitudes, and Sensations	237	L	Space and Time	545
G	Thought and Communication, Language and Grammar	297	M	Movement, Location, Travel, and Transport	603
			N	General and Abstract Terms	679

(*McArthur 1981: v*)

It also gives very useful examples for the learner. The user accesses a field by the word-index at the back of the lexicon; for example, if 'winning and losing' in sport is the area consulted, we find:

K108 *nouns* : **winning and losing**

win [C] *not fml* a success: *How many wins did he have?*

victory 1 [U (*in, over*)] the act of winning or state of having won (in sport, war, or in any kind of struggle): *The football team hoped for victory.* **2** [C (*in, over*)] a success in a fight, struggle, etc: *He had a narrow victory in the competition; he won by only a few points. The football team won some great victories. This army has won/gained many victories.*

triumph [U; C] *esp emot, fml & pomp* (a) great victory

defeat [C; U] the condition or an occasion of losing: *It's defeat; we've lost. How many defeats have they had this year?*

tie [C] an equality of results, in scores, etc: *The match ended in a tie, so we still don't know who's the winner of the competition. The result is a tie.*

draw [C] an occasion when two teams, persons, etc, end a game without either side winning; such a game: *The game was a draw. It's a draw!*

result [C *usu pl*] the announcement of a person's success or failure or of a match won or lost: *He heard the football result on the radio. How did you get on in the competition and when will you know your results?*

(*McArthur 1981:526*)

Other thesauruses such as the *Collins New World Thesaurus* (1981) simply arrange headwords alphabetically and provide lists of synonyms and antonyms. In the Collins thesaurus, non-core words in sets are cross-referred to core-words (see **4.1**), where lists of near synonyms appear, for example, the entries for 'skinny', 'slim' and 'thin'.

---

skinny, *mod.*—*Syn.* lean, gaunt, slender; see **thin** 2.

slim, *mod.*—*Syn.* slender, narrow, lank; see **thin** 2.

thin, *mod.* **1.** [Of little thickness]—*Syn.* flimsy, slim, slight, tenuous, attenuated, diaphanous, sheer, rare, sleazy, permeable, paper-thin, wafer-sliced; see also **transparent** 1. —*Ant.* thick*, heavy, coarse.
2. [Slender]—*Syn.* slim, lean, skinny, scraggy, lank, spare, gaunt, bony, wan, rangy, skeletal, scrawny, lanky, delicate, wasted, haggard, emaciated, rawboned, shriveled, wizened, rickety, spindling, pinched, starved; see also **dainty** 1. —*Ant.* fat*, obese, heavy.

(*Collins New World Thesaurus* 1981)

▶ ## TASK 112

Compare the entries for 'skinny' and 'slim' in the Collins thesaurus with the entries for the same words in McArthur's *Lexicon*. What extra sorts of information does the *Lexicon* give, and how important is it for learners? You may wish to refer back to the section on core vocabulary (**4.1**) for a discussion of similar examples.

---

skinny [Wa1] *usu derog* very thin: *Who is that tall skinny fellow? He has a good build except for rather skinny arms.* **-iness** [U]

slim [Wa1] **1** (of people) pleasantly thin; not fat: *She won't eat because she wants to be/stay slim. He has a fine slim muscular build.* **2** (*fig*) *infml* small: *He hopes to win the race but his chances are slim.* **-ness** [U]

(*McArthur 1981:56–7*)

(The symbol [U] means *uncountable noun*. [Wa1] means *takes the suffixes* -er and -est.)

10.2 Workbooks and reference activities

One of the problems teachers may encounter in encouraging their learners to use the excellent reference resources now available is that learners may not be experienced in using dictionaries, or else might be de-motivated by the complexities of the larger desk-dictionaries.

The most popular learners' dictionaries try to get round the problem by providing workbooks to accompany the dictionaries. *COBUILD*'s *Learning Real English* workbook (Fox and Kirby 1987) has exercises training the learner to understand the explanations, grammatical information, and pronunciation in the *COBUILD* dictionary. Owen (1989) is an expanded activity book for the *COBUILD* dictionary. The *Longman Dictionary Skills Handbook* (McAlpin 1988) also helps the learner through the jungle of information on headwords and offers guidance on how the dictionary presents meaning. Workbooks are a useful resource for the teacher who wishes to encourage good dictionary skills.

▶ TASK 113

Evaluate the two workbook extracts on compounds given overleaf. The first is from the *Learning Real English* workbook and the second from the *Longman Dictionary Skills Handbook*. Which is easier to understand, and which do you think your students would find most usable and motivating? Are labels such as *combination words* more helpful than talking about *compounds*? Which workbook gives the learner more of a sense of the *productivity* (the ability of the language to generate a wide range of forms from a small number of roots) of compounds?

Now consider these two-word entries from the list:

reading knowledge
reading room
space age
space research

English is full of combinations like this, and this dictionary has a lot of useful information about them.

Often these two-word combinations come as main entries in the normal alphabetical order. **Reading room** is a good example:

> **reading room, reading rooms**; also spelled N COUNT with a hyphen. A **reading room** is a quiet room in a library or museum where you can read and study. EG *He went down to the reading room of the British Museum.*

But sometimes you have to look a little more carefully. **Reading knowledge** comes in a paragraph under the main entry for **read**.

Space age has a main entry. **Space research** does not have an entry at all, but if you look carefully you will find it used as an example under the main entry for **space**.

In general, when a two-word expression has a main entry, it is because native speakers think of it as a 'compound', in other words, they think of it as if it were one word in meaning. But this is a very difficult area of English, and the language is constantly changing.

So, the advice here is, search around in all the possible places for two-word expressions.

(Fox and Kirby 1987:7)

6.4 Combination words

Some words are formed from a combination of two words, like this:

icebox   = a **box** for keeping food cold with **ice**
ice-cold = as **cold** as **ice**
ice age = an **age** when **ice** covered much of the Earth

1 Find these combination words in your dictionary. They all begin with **tooth.**

1 .... 2 .... 3 .... 4 ....

2 Make combination words to match these meanings, then check with your dictionary.

1 money made of paper = ...   5 work for students to do at home = ...

2 a boat used as a house = ...   6 the place of someone's birth = ...

3 a place where buses stop = ...   7 a bar that sells mainly wine = ...

4 as blue as the sky = ...   8 the time for going to bed = ...

3 Be careful of combination words which have an unexpected meaning! Try to match these ones with their correct meanings, then check with your dictionary.

1 **paper tiger** ( )   A a place where people can walk across a street safely
2 **dark horse** ( )   B a family member who has caused shame to the others
3 **zebra crossing** ( )   C an enemy that seems powerful but is not
4 **red herring** ( )   D a quiet person who may have hidden qualities
5 **black sheep** ( )   E something said to take attention away from a topic

When a word or a form of a word is often used to complete a combination word the dictionary tells you like this:

> **room**   *(often in comb.) ... the bathroom bedroom dining room...*
>   **5 -roomed** ... *a six-roomed house*

(McAlpin 1988:48)

Morgan and Rinvolucri (1986) offer classroom activities that are intended to encourage dictionary use and to be interactive and enjoyable. One such is a guessing game called 'Word dip':

F/5 Word dip

LEVEL	Elementary to Advanced
TIME	15–25 minutes
PREPARATION	Ensure that you have sufficient monolingual dictionaries available: one for each group of 2–4 players. Any monolingual dictionary will do, though for more advanced students the various learners' dictionaries may be less stimulating. Pocket dictionaries will not be adequate.
IN CLASS	1 Ask the students to form groups of 2–4 players each. Make sure each group has a dictionary.

2 Explain or demonstrate the game, then ask the groups to play one complete round. The game goes like this:

a. Player **A** opens the dictionary at random.

b. S/he chooses an unknown word defined on the pages open and tells the other player(s) what it is. (It may be helpful to insist that **A** both pronounces the word and spells it out. **A** may also give other information, such as part of speech, but *not* meaning.)

c. The other players then question **A** on the meaning of the word. **A** may answer only *yes* or *no*.

d. **A** scores a point if no one guesses the meaning within, say, twenty questions. Otherwise the first person to guess the meaning gets the point.

Two or three rounds should be the maximum to sustain interest: if the students wish to continue, then repeat the game on a later occasion.

(*Morgan and Rinvolucri 1986:96–7*)

Morgan and Rinvolucri's activities involve the use of dictionaries in enjoyable ways, but somewhat predictably, they still mostly emphasize the dictionary as a *decoding* tool rather than for encoding.

▶ TASK 114

How can one get round the problem of encouraging learners to use their dictionaries for encoding? Ideally, we would want students to use a good learner's dictionary, or a combinatory dictionary, to find out about appropriate grammatical patterns, collocations, and registerial information for words they are unsure of or only partially know, or to use a thesaurus or lexicon-type work for access to new lexical fields when they have meanings to express but lack the words to express them.

With other teachers, draw up a list of possible activities to encourage awareness of how the dictionary can be used for encoding purposes.

10.3 Conclusion

In Section Two we have looked at the implications of the descriptive base for vocabulary outlined in Section One, and at ways in which theory and description have found their way into teaching materials and reference works. We have also taken a brief look at what goes on in vocabulary lessons in the classroom, and considered the position of the learner, both in relation to the teacher and as an autonomous individual trying to master a foreign vocabulary. We have considered a wide range of exercises and activities designed to impart information concerning words, to train learners to be more effective in the vocabulary-learning exercise, and to use fully the resources available to assist them in their task.

We now turn to some further tasks for the exploration of vocabulary teaching.

Exploring vocabulary

11 Investigating vocabulary problems in the classroom

The tasks in this section are designed to explore further many of the issues dealt with in Section One and illustrated in Section Two. Their aim is to involve the teacher and, wherever possible, learners, in the investigation of vocabulary problems in the class. The tasks include those oriented towards the gathering of data for vocabulary learning, those concerned with observing the behaviour of teachers and learners in relation to vocabulary learning, and those concerned with materials and reference resources, and how these function in the classroom. They may also be seen as the basis for further investigations along similar lines, which teachers and students can carry out according to their own needs.

▶ TASK 115

Aim
To gather data for the teaching of word-formation principles.

Resources
A selection of current English language newspapers and magazines.

Procedure
1 Give some examples of derived words and compound words in English.
2 In pairs or in groups, the students collect data from the newspapers and magazines in the form of short clippings and text extracts which include derived words and compounds, and provide a brief context for them. About fifty items should be more than enough for sorting into categories.
3 Get the group as a whole to sort the data into types, according to their own criteria. They should be able to justify their choices.
4 Make sure the meanings of the items are clear, then set the class the task of adding new items as they are encountered over a fixed subsequent period.

Evaluation
1 What were the richest sources for data?
2 Which types of word-formation process seem to occur most often?
3 What problems were there in the classification of individual examples?
4 How might the collectively gathered data be used in future classroom activities?

► TASK 116

Aim
To gather data for the illustration of the notion of lexical density.

Resources
Sets of written rules for games such as table-tennis, board-games, card-games, etc. Tape-recorder.

Procedure
1 In advance, record pairs of native- or near-native-speakers where A explains to B how to play the game while actually performing the actions. Transcribe one sample extract from the tape.
2 In class, compare the vocabulary of the spoken extract with a corresponding passage in the written rules, noting the ratio of grammatical items to lexical items. Work out a figure for the lexical density of the two texts, as described in 5.3.

Evaluation
1 Does the comparison show any notable differences in the lexical density of the spoken and written texts?
2 Can the differences be readily categorized? For example, are there more pronouns in the spoken text, or more complex noun phrases in the written?
3 Is such data a useful basis for vocabulary materials designed to concentrate on differences between spoken and written language?
4 Would it be feasible to carry out the same experiment recording a group of non-native learners?

► TASK 117

Aim
To gather data to expand the students' range of colour vocabulary beyond the basic terms (e.g. 'red', 'green', 'brown') in an advanced level class.

Resources
Any realia where colour-names regularly occur (paint-charts, fashion magazines, advertisements, etc.). A good dictionary (e.g. the learners' dictionaries mentioned in 10.2), or a thesaurus or lexicon (e.g. McArthur 1981, *Chambers Twentieth Century Thesaurus* 1986, Kirkpatrick 1987).

Procedure
1 In groups, students choose three or four colour-names from the realia which they find unusual, interesting, or appealing in some way. They then check them in the dictionary, thesaurus, or lexicon and decide how unusual they are (e.g. if they do not appear at all, or if they are indicated as rare/literary).

2 In collaboration with the teacher, the word-lists are collated and sorted into names which are established colour-terms in the language, and names which are not.

Evaluation

1 Did the data yield sufficient examples of both established and non-established colour terms?

2 Did the sorting into 'established' and 'not established' groups help in the separation of vocabulary for receptive use and vocabulary for productive use?

3 Does the activity generate discussion of associations and connotations of words as well as their denotation?

▶ **TASK 118**

Aim
To explore the problems associated with teaching lexical sets.

Resources
Any appropriate visuals and/or realia.

Procedure
1 Design a presentation-phase of a lesson to present and illustrate the meaning of the following lexical set to a group of intermediate students:

hopes	*fears*	*expectations*	*plans*
ambitions	*worries*	*daydreams*	*wishes*

Use any kinds of resources you think appropriate (pictures, grids, as in 7.2, tape-recordings, etc.) to back up your presentation.

2 Try out the presentation with a group of intermediate learners.

Evaluation

1 How successful was the lesson in efficiently and economically presenting word meaning?

2 Were other differentiating factors brought to light (e.g. syntactic differences between the members of the set)?

3 How successful was the presentation in differentiating words that are often perceived as being very close in meaning to one another (e.g. 'hopes' and 'expectations')?

▶ **TASK 119**

Aim
To explore how far topic-based materials satisfy learners' perceived vocabulary needs.

Resources
Topic-based course material.

Procedure

1 Ask a group of adults to agree on a list of ten topics they would most like to cover on a ten-week language course. This can be done in small groups or pairs first, with the whole class pooling their results. They may need some examples, which you can give to them, so that everyone is quite clear that 'topic' here means 'talking' topics (e.g. sport, holidays, education), rather than 'language' topics (e.g. conditionals, prepositions).

2 Then, if there is time, ask each student to take one or two topics (depending on the size of the class), and list ten words in his or her L1 which he or she considers important words in connection with that topic. Where known, an English translation can be given alongside.

3 If possible, gather the results together, and, after the lesson, compare what the students consider to be important topics and words with what their course-material, or other material designed for their age and level, present as important.

Evaluation

1 Did the students find it easy to agree as to what were important topics for the course?

2 If they did the word exercise, is there a match between what they perceived to be important words and the sorts of words found in the course materials?

3 How reliable do you feel students are as informants in investigations such as these?

▶ **TASK 120**

Aim

Observing how new words are explained and received in class.

Resources

Word-list. A coded check-list for observation. Your class or that of a colleague who has agreed to be observed.

Procedure

1 Before a lesson, list twelve vocabulary items which you, or your colleague, intends to teach for *productive* use.

2 Draw up a check-list for types of word-explanation in class (see **6.3**). Use a simple code such as: (D) definition, (E) example phrase or sentence, (V) visual (drawing/mime), (S) synonym, (T) translation, and so on.

3 During the lesson, make notes on how each word was in fact explained, using the code. If more than one method was used for a particular word, note each one.

Evaluation

1 Did the code cover all the ways that arose for explaining word-meanings?

2 Did some words require more than one method of explanation? If they did, which ones were they, and why do you think this was necessary?

3 How well did the initial word-list predict the learners' state of knowledge? Were any of the words chosen already known or had they been encountered before by some or all of the students?

▶ **TASK 121**

Aim

To assess the types of contributions students make to the establishing of the meaning of new words in class.

Resources

Tape-recorder. Your class, or that of a colleague.

Procedure

1 Tape-record a section of a lesson in which the teacher is explaining new words.

2 Listen to the recording and note occasions where students contribute to the establishing of meaning, by asking questions, offering definitions, guessing, and so on.

3 Categorize the student contributions into types.

Evaluation

1 If you can, refer back to the intuitive list you drew up for Task 99; does the recorded data bear out your intuitions as to how students behave?

2 Is there a wide range of types of student contribution on the tape? If the range is restricted, could there be a case for some sort of training in strategies for getting at the meanings of new words?

3 Are the 'better' learners in the class performing notably differently from the weaker ones in this area?

▶ **TASK 122**

Aim

To explore the role of repetition of new words in the vocabulary lesson.

Resources

Tape-recorder. Your class, or that of a colleague.

Procedure

1 Tape-record thirty minutes of a vocabulary lesson.

2 Listen to the recording and make some rough calculations of how often new words are *repeated* (by both teacher *and* students). Note also any new words that only occur once.

Evaluation

1 Do any new words occur only once?

2 What sorts of words seem to get the most repetitions?

3 What seem to be the reasons for the repetitions?

4 Are the repetitions prompted by the teacher or the students?

▶ TASK 123

Aim

To explore the relationship between word-association and learners' lexical development.

Resources

A list of test items.

Procedure

1 Draw up a list of six to eight words to be used as stimuli in a simple word-association test. Try to vary the test items, to include:

– at least one grammar/function word (e.g. preposition, pronoun).

– one or two items from the everyday physical environment (e.g. 'table', 'car').

– a relatively uncommon or low-frequency word but one which your students will nonetheless know (this will depend on the group's level: elementary-level students might require a word like 'drink', but an advanced group can probably cope with a word like 'surrender'; your own experience will tell you what is suitable).

– a mix of word-classes (e.g. noun, adjective, verb).

2 Deliver the test to the class, asking them to write down the very first word that occurs to them when each item is heard.

3 Gather in the results and see if any patterns emerge from the responses.

Evaluation

1 Does such a word-association test tell you anything about how your learners are making mental links between words they have learnt?

2 At lower levels, are phonological similarities playing an important role?

3 Do the results bear out the characteristic types of response discussed in **3.2**?

▶ TASK 124

Aim

To explore learners' awareness of the translatability of different senses of polysemous words (see **2.4**).

Resources

Access to good learners' dictionaries in class.

Procedure

1 Recalling Kellerman's experiments (see **2.4**) concerning his Dutch students' intuitive feel for which meanings of polysemous Dutch words would be most/least likely to translate directly into English, set up a similar experiment with your students.

2 Take a word which is likely to be polysemous in the students' L1(s). Words like 'head', 'hand', 'eye', 'take', 'stand', 'lie', etc. are likely to be polysemous in many languages.

3 Get the class in pairs, groups, or as a whole class (depending on the nationality mix of the class), to make notes on as many different meanings as they can think of for the literal translation of the chosen word in their L1. They should then write a short sentence in their L1 to illustrate each meaning they have listed for the word.

4 Get them to 'vote' as to how likely it is that each of their sentences will translate directly into English using the key word in English.

5 Try translating some of their sentences with them to see how well their intuition matches the facts.

6 Ask them to check in a good learner's dictionary to see how far the different senses given for the English word overlap with the senses of the L1 literal translation.

Evaluation

1 Do the results of the experiment confirm Kellerman's findings?

2 Are students able to reflect on their own L1 objectively and produce examples of different senses for polysemous words?

3 Does the activity have any practical spin-off in raising the students' awareness of the learner's dictionary as an *encoding* tool (see **10.1**)?

▶ **TASK 125**

Aim
To test retention of new words.

Resources
Word lists from three consecutive lessons with the same class.

Procedure

1 During three consecutive lessons with the same group, make a list of as many as possible of the vocabulary items that have been dealt with in class. If possible, sort these into those directly taught for productive use, those taught for receptive use, and those which just cropped up without planning.

2 Devise a simple test (e.g. multiple choice, gap-filling, or sentence completion) involving twenty items, representing the different types in 1 above.

3 Without warning them, administer the test to the class one week after the last of the three lessons, record the results, then administer the same test after another three weeks have passed, then again after a further six weeks have passed. Record the results.

Evaluation
1 What do the test scores tell you about how the words have been retained?
2 Are some types of words more readily retained than others?
3 Is there a correlation between the way the word occurred in class (productive/receptive/just cropped up) and how well it is retained?

▶ TASK 126

Aim
To explore students' lexical communication strategies.

Resources
Tape-recorder.

Procedure
1 Observe, and if possible record, three or four pair- or group-work sessions in your class in which students are obliged to speak English with one another.
2 Note occasions when lexical difficulties occur.
3 Note whether students get over the difficulties by using any of the following strategies:
   – helping each other
   – resorting to an L1 translation
   – paraphrase or circumlocution
   – asking the teacher for help
   – any other strategy

Evaluation
1 Did lexical difficulties occur at all? If so, what types?
2 Were the difficulties satisfactorily resolved?
3 Do students display a natural tendency to help one another out of difficulties?
4 Does the activity suggest any need for training or awareness-raising in communication strategies?

▶ TASK 127

Aim
To investigate the discourse-level vocabulary skills of intermediate and advanced learners.

Resources
Written data from learners (discursive essays) at intermediate or advanced level. Materials used by the same learners.

Procedure
In relation to the discussion of vocabulary and discourse in **4.3**, analyse ten discursive essays by intermediate or advanced level students. Consider whether the following features are present:

– lexical cohesion in the form of synonyms, hyponyms, etc. over clause- and sentence-boundaries
– discourse-signalling words
– modal words (modal verbs *and* lexical modals)
– expressive modifiers

Evaluation
1 Were some or all of the discourse features present?

2 Were some discourse features handled better (with fewer errors or inappropriate usages) than others?

3 Does the data suggest that discourse level vocabulary skills are transferred automatically from L1, or that such skills might need direct intervention by the teacher to help them develop in L2?

4 Do any of the materials the class uses present or give practice in vocabulary at the discourse level?

► **TASK 128**

Aim
To investigate students' use of dictionaries.

Resources
Questionnaire. Class of intermediate or upper-intermediate learners.

Procedure
Refer to your findings from Task 109 and devise a questionnaire consisting of not more than twenty items, with the aim of finding out how your students use dictionaries. Things you may wish to find out might include whether they use monolingual or bilingual dictionaries, whether they use them for encoding or only for decoding, whether they ever use them for grammatical or phonological information, what types of words they look up, and so on. Administer the questionnaire to an intermediate or upper-intermediate class.

Evaluation
1 What patterns emerge from the responses? Is one type of dictionary more popular than others?

2 Is there a tendency to regard dictionaries as decoding instruments only?

3 Do the results point to a need for some sort of dictionary training in class? What should such training be specifically aimed at?

4 Would the workbooks and reference activities illustrated in **10.2** go some way towards improving students' dictionary skills?

▶ ## TASK 129

Aim
To explore whether students organize their vocabulary notes efficiently.

Resources
Students' own vocabulary notebooks.

Procedure
1 With their permission, borrow the vocabulary notebooks of your class (this is probably best done two or three at a time) and observe what sorts of notes they have taken.

2 Interview a selection of students and find out how they approach note-taking for vocabulary.

Evaluation
1 Are your students' notes similar to those illustrated in **9.3**?

2 How far do the students' notes reflect the methods you use in class to explain the words they have noted during lessons?

3 How often do the students simply write translations?

4 What evidence is there that students are entering words they have come across outside the classroom?

5 Does the investigation suggest any need for you to intervene and advise on note-taking?

▶ ## TASK 130

Aim
To explore individualized vocabulary learning.

Resources
One index-card per student.

Procedure
1 Set the class the task of recording *one* new English word per day for ten days. The words should be ones that they feel, for any reason whatsoever, are special, memorable, interesting, or in some other way personally engaging for them. Each student records his or her ten words on an index-card.

2 Collect all the cards together at the end of the ten-day period.

3 Analyse the lists to see if any patterns emerge.

Evaluation

1 Is there any overall pattern in the types of words chosen? Are there any obvious reasons why individuals have chosen their particular words?

2 Could the words be used as the basis for a vocabulary test, and if so, what sorts of results might one expect?

3 Could the words be used as the basis for vocabulary activities for the class as a whole?

Glossary

antonymy: relation of oppositeness of meaning (e.g. 'alive'/'dead', 'hot'/ 'cold').

collocation: the likelihood of co-occurrence between words. It is very likely that 'blonde' will occur with 'hair', but unlikely that it will occur with 'wallpaper'; 'blonde' and 'hair' are said to *collocate*.

compounds: items formed by combining two or more words (e.g. 'dustbin', 'windscreen-wiper').

concordance: a list showing the immediate environment in which a given word occurs in a number of different texts.

core vocabulary: words of neutral meaning in any lexical set; core words collocate more readily with a wide range of words, they may be used in a wider range of registers, and are usually involved in the definition of non-core members of their set.

decoding: finding the meanings of unknown words.

derived words: words formed by using prefixes and/or suffixes (e.g. *de*human*ize*).

encoding: finding words to fit desired meanings.

hyponymy: relation of inclusion (e.g. 'tulip' includes the meaning 'flower'). 'Tulip' is a hyponym of 'flower'.

idiom: a lexical item (usually a phrase or clause) whose meaning cannot be derived from the sum of its parts (e.g. 'to fly off the handle', meaning 'to lose one's temper').

lexical density: the ratio of the number of lexical words to the number of grammatical words in any text.

lexical item: any item which functions as a single unit in the lexicon. 'Box' is a lexical item. 'Jack-in-the-box' is also a lexical item, though it consists of four words. 'Watch', 'watching', 'watches', and 'watched' can be represented as one lexical item WATCH, which has a *scatter* of four different forms.

lexical variation: a measure of the number of new, different words which occur in any given stretch of text, as opposed to repeated words.

lexicon: the vocabulary of a language, its words. Also used as a term for a dictionary, thesaurus, or word-list.

lexis: vocabulary

meronymy: part–whole relation; 'wheel' is a meronym of 'bicycle'.

multi-word unit (MWU): any compound, phrase, clause, sentence, or segment of text that functions as a single lexical item (e.g. 'by and large', 'cool, calm, and collected').

paradigmatic: concerned with how each word in a text reflects a *choice* from a number of possible words. Often thought of as the 'vertical' axis of text.

procedural vocabulary: vocabulary used to explain other words, to structure and organize their meaning. In the sentence 'a rose is a type of flower', 'type' is a procedural word.

prototype: the most typical or central example of a class of things. For British people, a 'robin' is more prototypical of the class 'bird' than 'heron' or 'albatross'.

range: the list of items any lexical item may collocate with. The range of 'auburn' includes 'hair', 'locks', and 'tresses', but probably very few other items in English.

semantic field: an area of meaning covered by a set of related lexical items (e.g. 'modes of transport' would include a set of names of vehicles and ways of travelling).

synonymy: relation of sameness of meaning.

syntagmatic: concerned with how words *combine* to form text. Often thought of as the 'horizontal' axis of text.

Further Reading

The books and papers listed in the bibliography may be consulted for further discussion and illustration of the issues covered in Sections One and Two. The following is a selection of other sources readers might like to consult for general background reading on vocabulary, and as sources of reference for wider reading.

Carter, R. A. 1987. *Vocabulary*. London: Allen and Unwin.
Carter's book ranges widely over issues in vocabulary, and, although there is a small amount of overlap with Carter and McCarthy (1988), it is an indispensable source of general background reading.

Jackson, H. 1988. *Words and their Meaning*. London: Longman.
A good, clear introduction to vocabulary studies; of particular interest to lexicographers.

Lyons, J. 1981. *Language, Meaning and Context*. London: Fontana Paperbacks.
Contains a good, easily readable introduction to lexical semantics.

Meara, P. 1980. 'Vocabulary acquisition: a neglected aspect of language learning.' *Language Teaching and Linguistics: Abstracts* 13:221–46. Reprinted in V. Kinsella (ed.): *Surveys 1*. Cambridge: Cambridge University Press 1982: 100–26.
This survey is an excellent source of further reading on vocabulary, especially from the psycholinguistic angle.

Meara, P. (ed.) 1983 and 1987. *Vocabulary in a Second Language*. 2 vols. London: Centre for Information on Language Teaching and Research. These two volumes of bibliography contain short abstracts of each reference listed and are an invaluable source of further reading.

Regional English Language Centre. 1980. *Guidelines for Vocabulary Teaching. RELC Journal Supplement 3*. Singapore: RELC.
A collection of papers by various authors, with a very practical orientation.

Bibliography

Aitchison, J. 1987. *Words in the Mind: An Introduction to the Mental Lexicon*. Oxford: Basil Blackwell.

Alexander, R. J. 1978. 'Fixed expressions in English: a linguistic, psycholinguistic and didactic study.' *Anglistik und Englischunterricht* 6: 171–88.

Alexander, R. J. 1984. 'Fixed expressions in English: reference books and the teacher.' *English Language Teaching Journal* 38/2: 127–32.

Allen, V. F. 1983. *Techniques in Teaching Vocabulary*. Oxford: Oxford University Press.

Atkinson, R. C. 1972. 'Optimizing the learning of a second language vocabulary.' *Journal of Experimental Psychology* 96: 124–9.

Bauer, L. 1983. *English Word-formation*. Cambridge: Cambridge University Press.

Béjoint, H. 1981. 'The foreign student's use of monolingual English dictionaries. A study of language needs and reference skills.' *Applied Linguistics* 2/3: 207–22.

Benson, J. D. and Greaves, W. S. 1981. 'Field of discourse: theory and application.' *Applied Linguistics* 2/1: 45–55.

Benson, M., E. Benson, and R. Ilson. 1986. *The BBI Combinatory Dictionary of English*. Amsterdam: John Benjamins.

Benson, M. and E. Benson. 1988. 'Trying out a new dictionary.' *TESOL Quarterly* 22/2: 340–5.

Blum-Kulka, S. and E. Levenston. 1983. 'Universals of lexical simplification' in C. Færch and G. Kasper (eds.): *Strategies in Interlanguage Communication*. London: Longman, 1983.

Bolinger, D. 1976. 'Meaning and memory.' *Forum Linguisticum* 1/1: 1–14.

Browne, V. 1987. *Odd Pairs and False Friends: dizionario di false analogie e ambigue affinita fra Inglese e Italiano*. Bologna: Zanichelli.

Brutten, S. 1981. 'An analysis of student and teacher indications of vocabulary difficulty.' *RELC Journal* 12/1: 66–71.

Bygate, M. 1987. *Speaking*. In the series: *Language Teaching: A Scheme for Teacher Education*. Oxford: Oxford University Press.

Carrell, P. L. 1987. 'Content and formal schemata in ESL reading.' *TESOL Quarterly* 21/3: 461–81.

Carrell, P. and J. Eisterhold. 1983. 'Schema theory and ESL reading pedagogy.' *TESOL Quarterly* 17/4: 553–73.

Carter, R. A. 1987. 'Is there a core vocabulary?: some implications for language teaching.' *Applied Linguistics* 8/2: 178–93.

Carter, R. A. and M. N. Long. 1987. *The Web of Words*. Cambridge: Cambridge University Press.

Carter, R. and M. J. McCarthy. (eds.) 1988. *Vocabulary and Language Teaching*. London: Longman.

Chaffin, R., D. J. Herrman, and M. Winston. 1988. 'An empirical taxonomy of part-whole relations: effects of part-whole relation type on relation identification.' *Language and Cognitive Processes* 3/1: 17–48.

Chambers Twentieth Century Thesaurus. 1986. Edinburgh: Chambers.

Channell, J. 1981. 'Applying semantic theory to vocabulary teaching.' *English Language Teaching Journal* 35/2: 115–22.

Channell, J. 1988. 'Psycholinguistic considerations in the study of L2 vocabulary acquisition' in Carter and McCarthy 1988.

Chaudron, C. 1982. 'Vocabulary elaboration in teachers' speech to L2 learners.' *Studies in Second Language Acquisition* 4/2: 170–80.

Chaudron, C. 1983. 'Foreigner talk in the classroom—an aid to learning?' in H. W. Seliger and M. Long (eds.): *Classroom Oriented Research in Second Language Acquisition*. Rowley, Mass.: Newbury House, 1983.

Channell, J. 1981. 'Applying semantic theory to vocabulary teaching.' *English Language Teaching Journal* 35/2: 115–22.

Collins COBUILD English Language Dictionary. 1987. London and Glasgow: Collins.

Collins New World Thesaurus. 1981. London and Glasgow: Collins.

Collinson, W. E. 1939. 'Comparative synonymics: some principles and illustrations.' *Transactions of the Philological Society*: 54–77.

Conybeare, M. A. 1986. 'A database-aided exploration of some characteristics of computer terminology.' Unpublished MA dissertation, University of Lancaster.

Cook, G. 1989. *Discourse*. In the series: *Language Teaching: A Scheme for Teacher Education*. Oxford: Oxford University Press.

Coulthard, M. 1985. *An Introduction to Discourse Analysis*. New edition. London: Longman.

Cowie, A. P. and R. Mackin. 1975. *Oxford Dictionary of Current Idiomatic English. Volume 1*. Oxford: Oxford University Press.

Cowie, A. P., R. Mackin, and I. R. McCaig. 1983. *Oxford Dictionary of Current Idiomatic English. Volume 2*. Oxford: Oxford University Press.

Cowie, A. P. 1988. 'Prefabricated Language and Journalistic Prose.' Paper given at the Annual Meeting of the British Association for Applied Linguistics, University of Exeter, 1988.

Cruse, D. A. 1975. 'Hyponymy and lexical hierarchies.' *Archivum Linguisticum* VI: 26–31.

Cruse, D. A., 1986. *Lexical Semantics*. Cambridge: Cambridge University Press.

Crystal, D. and D. Davy. 1975. *Advanced Conversational English*. London: Longman.

Donley, M. 1974. 'The role of structural semantics in expanding and activating the vocabulary of the advanced learner: the example of the homophone.' *Audio-Visual Language Journal* 12/2: 81–9.

Durrell, L. 1982. 'The Death of General Uncebunke' from *Collected Poems by Lawrence Durrell*. London: Faber and Faber.

X **Ellis, G.** and **B. Sinclair.** 1989. *Learning to Learn English.* Cambridge: Cambridge University Press.

Ellis, M. and **P. Ellis.** 1983. *Shades of Meaning.* Walton-on-Thames: Nelson.

Færch, C., K. Haastrup, and **R. Phillipson.** 1984. *Learner Language and Language Learning.* Copenhagen: Gyldendal.

Fowler, W. S. 1987. *The Right Word.* Walton-on-Thames: Nelson.

Fox, G. and **D. Kirby.** 1987. *Learning Real English with Collins-COBUILD English Language Dictionary.* London and Glasgow: Collins.

X **Fox, J.** and **J. Mahood.** 1982. 'Lexicons and the ELT materials writer.' *English Language Teaching Journal* 36/2: 125–9.

Gairns, R. and **S. Redman.** 1986. *Working with Words.* Cambridge: Cambridge University Press.

Gibbs, R. W. 1986. 'Skating on thin ice: literal meaning and understanding idioms in conversation.' *Discourse Processes* 9/1: 17–30.

Godman, A. and **E. M. F. Payne.** 1979. *Longman Dictionary of Scientific Usage.* London: Longman.

Halliday, M. A. K. 1966. 'Lexis as a linguistic level' in C. E. Bazell, J. C. Catford, M. A. K. Halliday, and R. H. Robins (eds.): *In Memory of J. R. Firth.* London: Longman, 1966.

Halliday, M. A. K. 1978. *Language as Social Semiotic.* London: Edward Arnold.

Halliday, M. A. K. and **R. Hasan.** 1976. *Cohesion in English.* London: Longman.

Heaton, J. B. and **N. D. Turton.** 1987. *Longman Dictionary of Common Errors.* London: Longman.

Henning, G. H. 1973. 'Remembering foreign language vocabulary: acoustic and semantic parameters.' *Language Learning* 23/2: 185–96.

Hermerén, L. 1978. *On Modality in English: A Study of the Semantics of the Modals.* Lund Studies in English 53. Lund: CWK Gleerup.

Hoey, M. 1983. *On the Surface of Discourse.* London: Allen and Unwin.

Hofland, K. and **S. Johansson.** 1982. *Word Frequencies in British and American English.* Bergen: The Norwegian Computing Centre for the Humanities.

Holmes, J. 1983. 'Speaking English with the appropriate degree of conviction' in C. Brumfit (ed.): *Learning and Teaching Languages for Communication: Applied Linguistic Perspectives.* London: CILT, 1983.

Hutchinson, T. and **A. Waters.** 1981. 'Performance and competence in English for specific purposes.' *Applied Linguistics* 2/1: 56–69.

Jain, M. P. 1981. 'On meaning in the foreign learner's dictionary.' *Applied Linguistics* 2/3: 274–86.

Johansson, S. 1978. *Some Aspects of the Vocabulary of Learned and Scientific English.* Gothenburg: Acta Universitatis Gothoburgensis.

X **Jordan, M. P.** 1984. *Rhetoric of Everyday English Texts.* London: Allen and Unwin.

Katz, J. J. and **J. A. Fodor.** 1963. 'The structure of a semantic theory.' *Language* 39: 170–210.

Kellerman, E. 1986. 'An eye for an eye: crosslinguistic constraints on the development of the L2 lexicon' in E. Kellerman and M. Sharwood Smith: *Crosslinguistic Influence in Second Language Acquisition*. Oxford: Pergamon Press, 1986.

Kelly, P. 1986. 'Solving the vocabulary retention problem.' *ITL Review of Applied Linguistics* 74: 1–16.

Kirkpatrick, B. (ed.) 1987. *Roget's Thesaurus of English Words and Phrases*. London: Longman.

Kucera, H. and **W. N. Francis.** 1967. *Computational Analysis of Present Day American English*. Providence, RI: Brown University Press.

Labov, W. 1973. 'The boundaries of words and their meanings' in C. N. Bailey and R. Shuy (eds.): *New Ways of Analysing Variation in English*. Washington, DC: Georgetown University Press, 1973.

Lakoff, G. and **M. Johnson.** 1980. *Metaphors We Live By*. Chicago and London: University of Chicago Press.

Langacker, R. W. 1987. *Foundations of Cognitive Grammar. Volume 1*. Stanford, Calif.: Stanford University Press.

Laufer, B. 1981. 'A problem in vocabulary learning: synophones.' *English Language Teaching Journal* 35/3: 294–300.

Leech, G. 1981. *Semantics*. Second edition. Harmondsworth: Penguin.

Lehrer, A. 1974. *Semantic Fields and Lexical Structure*. Amsterdam: North Holland Publishing Company.

Lehrer, A. 1985. 'Is semantics perception-driven or network-driven?' *Australian Journal of Linguistics* 5: 197–207.

Liu, N. and **I. S. P. Nation.** 1985. 'Factors affecting guessing vocabulary in context.' *RELC Journal* 16/1: 33–42.

Longman Dictionary of Contemporary English. New edition 1987. London: Longman.

Longman Dictionary of English Idioms. 1979. London: Longman.

Low, G. D. 1988. 'On teaching metaphor.' *Applied Linguistics* 9/2: 125–47.

Lyons, J. 1977. *Semantics. Volumes I and II*. Cambridge: Cambridge University Press.

Makkai, A. 1978. 'Idiomaticity as a language universal' in J. H. Greenberg (ed.): *Universals of Human Language, Volume 3: Word Structure*. Stanford, Calif.: Stanford University Press, 1978.

McAlpin, J. 1988. *Longman Dictionary Skills Handbook*. London: Longman.

McArthur, T. 1981. *Longman Lexicon of Contemporary English*. London: Longman.

McCarthy, M. J. (in press) *Discourse Analysis for Language Teachers*. Cambridge: Cambridge University Press.

McCarthy, M. J., A. MacLean, and **P. O'Malley.** 1985. *Proficiency Plus: Grammar, Lexis, Discourse*. Oxford: Basil Blackwell.

Medani, A. 1988. 'Vocabulary learning strategies of "good" and "poor" learners' in P. Meara (ed.): *Beyond Words*. London: CILT, 1989.

Michea, R. 1953. 'Mots fréquents et mots disponibles.' *Les Langues Modernes* 47: 338–44.

Micro-OCP. 1988. (Text Analysis Program) Oxford: Oxford University Press.

Miller, G. A. 1978. 'Semantic relations among words' in M. Halle, J. Bresnan, and G. A. Miller (eds.): *Linguistic Theory and Psychological Reality.* Cambridge, Mass.: MIT Press.

Moore, T. and **C. Carling.** 1982. *Understanding Language: Towards a Post-Chomskyan Linguistics.* London: The Macmillan Press.

Morgan, J. and **M. Rinvolucri.** 1986. *Vocabulary.* Oxford: Oxford University Press.

Nation, I. S. P. 1982. 'Beginning to learn foreign vocabulary: a review of the research.' *RELC Journal* 13/1: 14–36.

Nation, I. S. P. and **J. Coady** 1988. 'Vocabulary and reading' in Carter and McCarthy 1988.

Nattinger, J. 1988. 'Some current trends in vocabulary teaching' in Carter and McCarthy 1988.

Nesi, H. 1988. 'Which dictionary? A review of the leading learners' dictionaries.' Paper given at the 22nd International IATEFL Conference, University of Edinburgh, 1988.

Nida, E. A. 1975. *Componential Analysis of Meaning.* The Hague: Mouton.

Oxford Advanced Learner's Dictionary. Fourth edition 1989. Oxford: Oxford University Press.

Owen, C. 1989. *Collins-COBUILD Essential English Dictionary Workbook.* London and Glasgow: Collins.

Palmer, F. R. 1981. *Semantics.* Second edition. Cambridge: Cambridge University Press.

Pearson, P. D. and **D. D. Johnson.** 1978. *Teaching Reading Comprehension.* New York: Holt, Rinehart and Winston.

Pender, J. 1988. 'An investigation into the treatment of vocabulary with intermediate level students in the monolingual classroom.' Unpublished MA dissertation, University of Birmingham.

Qun, H. 1988. 'Chinese students' difficulties in reading the English press.' Unpublished MA dissertation, University of Birmingham.

Redman, S. and **R. Ellis.** 1989. *A Way with Words. Book 1.* Cambridge: Cambridge University Press.

Redman S. and **R. Ellis.** 1990. *A Way with Words. Book 2.* Cambridge: Cambridge University Press.

Richards, J. C. 1974. 'Word lists: problems and prospects.' *RELC Journal* 5/2: 69–84.

Richards, J. C. 1976. 'The role of vocabulary teaching.' *TESOL Quarterly* 10/1: 77–89.

Richards, J. C. and **T. S. Rodgers.** 1986. *Approaches and Methods in Language Teaching.* Cambridge: Cambridge University Press.

Robinson, P. 1988. 'A Hallidayan framework for vocabulary teaching: an approach to organising the lexical content of an EFL syllabus.' *International Review of Applied Linguistics* XXVI/3: 229–38.

Rosch, E. H. 1973. 'On the internal structure of perceptual and semantic categories' in T. E. Moore (ed.): *Cognitive Development and the Acquisition of Language.* New York: Academic Press.

Rudzka, B., J. Channell, P. Ostyn, and Y. Putseys. 1981. *The Words You Need*. London: Macmillan.

Rudzka, B., J. Channell, P. Ostyn, and Y. Putseys. 1985. *More Words You Need*. London: Macmillan.

Seal, B. 1987. *Vocabulary Builder 1*. London: Longman.

Sim, D. D. and B. Laufer-Dvorkin. 1984. *Vocabulary Development*. London and Glasgow: Collins.

Sinclair, J. McH. 1987. 'Collocation: a progress report' in R. Steel and T. Threadgold (eds.): *Language Topics: Essays in Honour of Michael Halliday*. Amsterdam: John Benjamins, 1987.

Sinclair, J. McH. 1988. 'Sense and structure in lexis' in J. D. Benson, M. J. Cummings, and W. S. Greaves (eds.): *Linguistics in a Systemic Perspective*. Amsterdam: John Benjamins, 1988.

Sinclair, J. McH. and A. Renouf. 1988. 'A lexical syllabus for language learning' in Carter and McCarthy 1988.

Soars, J. and L. Soars. 1986. *Headway Intermediate*. Oxford: Oxford University Press.

Soars, J. and L. Soars. 1987. *Headway Upper Intermediate*. Oxford: Oxford University Press.

Stubbs, M. 1986. ' "A matter of prolonged fieldwork": notes towards a modal grammar of English.' *Applied Linguistics* 7/1: 1–25.

Summers, D. 1988. 'The role of dictionaries in language learning' in Carter and McCarthy 1988.

Svartvik, J. and R. Quirk. 1980. *A Corpus of English Conversation*. Lund: Liberläromedel.

Swan, M. and C. Walter. 1984. *The Cambridge English Course. Book 1*. Cambridge: Cambridge University Press.

Swan, M. and C. Walter. 1985. *The Cambridge English Course. Book 2*. Cambridge: Cambridge University Press.

Taylor, L. 1986. 'Vocabulary acquisition: a study of teacher and learner strategies.' Unpublished MA dissertation, University of Birmingham.

The New Encyclopaedia Britannica. Fifteenth edition 1985. Chicago and London: Encyclopaedia Britannica Inc.

Thomas, B. J. 1986. *Intermediate Vocabulary*. London: Edward Arnold.

Tomaszczyk, J. 1981. 'Bilingual pedagogical lexicography.' *Applied Linguistics* 2/3: 287–96.

Trollope, A. 1857. *Barchester Towers*. London: T. Nelson and Sons.

Ure, J. 1971. 'Lexical density and register differentiation' in G. E. Perren and J. L. M. Trim (eds.) *Applications of Linguistics*. Cambridge: Cambridge University Press.

Wagner, M. J. and G. Tilney. 1983. 'The effect of "superlearning techniques" on the vocabulary acquisition and alpha brainwave production of language learners.' *TESOL Quarterly* 17/1: 5–17.

West, M. P. 1953. *A General Service List of English Words*. London: Longman.

Widdowson, H. G. 1978. *Teaching Language as Communication*. Oxford: Oxford University Press.

Widdowson, H. G. 1983. *Learning Purpose and Language Use*. Oxford: Oxford University Press.

Willis, D. and **J. Willis.** 1988. *Collins COBUILD English Course. Book 1*. London and Glasgow: Collins.

Xiaolong, L. 1988. 'Effects of contextual cues on inferring and remembering meanings of new words.' *Applied Linguistics* 9/4: 402–13.

Zimmermann, R. 1987. 'Form-oriented and content-oriented lexical errors in L2 learners.' *International Review of Applied Linguistics* XXV/1: 55–67.

Index

Entries relate to Sections One, Two, and Three of the text, and to the glossary. References to the glossary are indicated by 'g' after the page number. Titles of publications, and also foreign words, are given in italics.

Acknowledgements

The publishers would like to thank the following for their permission to reproduce material that falls within their copyright:

Acta Universitatis Gothoburgensis for a table from *Some Aspects of the Vocabulary of Learned and Scientific English* by S. Johansson (1978).

The British Association for Applied Linguistics for an extract from *Beyond Words* (1989) by P. Meara.

Cambridge University Press for extracts from *Working with Words* (1986) by R. Gairns and S. Redman, *Learning to Learn English* (1989) by G. Ellis and B. Sinclair, and *A Way with Words, Book 1* (1989) and *A Way with Words, Book 2* (1990) by S. Redman and R. Ellis.

Collins ELT for extracts from *Vocabulary Development* (1984) by D. D. Sim and B. Laufer-Dvorkin, *Collins COBUILD English Language Dictionary* (1987), and *Learning Real English with Collins COBUILD English Language Dictionary* (1987).

Edward Arnold for an extract from *Intermediate Vocabulary* (1986) by B. J. Thomas.

Encyclopaedia Britannica Inc. for an extract from 'Endocrine systems' in *Encyclopaedia Britannica*, Fifteenth edition (1985).

Faber and Faber Ltd, and Viking Penguin (a division of Penguin Books USA Inc.), for an extract from 'The Death of General Uncebunke' from *Collected Poems* copyright © 1980 by Lawrence Durrell.

Holt, Rinehart and Winston Inc. for a figure from *Teaching Reading Comprehension* by P. David Pearson and Dale D. Johnson copyright © 1978.

John Benjamins BV for an extract from the *BBI Combinatory Dictionary of English* (1986) edited by M. Benson, E. Benson, and R. Ilson (1986).

John Rodda for an extract from his article on boxing published in the *Guardian* on 23 September 1988.

Longman Group UK for extracts from *Advanced Conversational English* (1975) by D. Crystal and D. Davy, *Longman Dictionary of Contemporary English* (1978 and 1987 editions), *Vocabulary Builder 1* (1978) by B. Seal, *Longman Dictionary of English Idioms* (1979), *A Corpus of English Conversation* (1980) by J. Svartvik and R. Quirk, *Longman Lexicon of Contemporary English* (1981) by T. McArthur, and *Longman Dictionary Skills Handbook* (1988) by J. McAlpin.

Macmillan Publishers Ltd for extracts from *The Words You Need* (1981) by B. Rudzka, J. Channell, Y. Putseys, and P. Ostyn.

Nicola Zanichelli S.p.A. for an extract from *Odd Pairs and False Friends* (1987) by Virginia Browne.

Syndication International for an extract from an article by John Jackson published in the *Daily Mirror* on 23 September 1988.

The *Observer* newspaper for extracts from an article published on 11 September 1988.

The Research Foundation of the State University of New York for a table from *Cognitive Development and the Acquisition of Language* (1973) edited by T. E. Moore.

The University of Birmingham, on behalf of the many authors who allowed their works to be included in the Birmingham Corpus of English Texts, for two excerpts.

The University of London Institute of Education for two extracts from *A General Service List of English Words* (1953) by M. P. West.

The publishers would also like to thank the following Oxford University Press authors and editors for agreeing to the reproduction of extracts from their publications:

Virginia French Allen for extracts from *Techniques in Teaching Vocabulary* (1983).

Joanna Channell for a table from 'Applying semantic theory to vocabulary teaching' (1981) published in the *English Language Teaching Journal* 35/2.

A. P. Cowie for an extract from the *Oxford Advanced Learner's Dictionary of Current English*, Fourth edition (1989).

A. P. Cowie and R. Mackin for an extract from the *Oxford Dictionary of Current Idiomatic English*, *Volume 1* (1975).

John Morgan and Mario Rinvolucri for extracts from *Vocabulary* (1986) published in the series Resource Books for Teachers.

John and Liz Soars for extracts from *Headway Intermediate* (1986) and *Headway Upper-Intermediate* (1987).